# Rent to Wealth: The Proven Path to Financial Freedom through Rental Property

# Introduction

"Real estate rental properties have long been a popular investment option for those looking to achieve financial freedom. The ability to generate passive income and build wealth over time has made rental properties an attractive option for investors. However, managing a rental business can be complex, and there are many factors to consider when it comes to maximizing rental income, managing cash flow, and understanding the tax and legal implications of owning rental properties.

In this book, we will cover topics such as financing your rental business, managing cash flow, property management, long-term strategies, real estate market trends, legal and tax implications, insurance, scaling your rental business and creating passive income streams. We will also discuss ways to minimize risks, costs, and adapt to changes in the market.

Whether you're a first-time landlord or an experienced property manager, this book provides the knowledge and tools needed to build a profitable and sustainable rental business. With the strategies and best practices outlined in this book, landlords and property managers can achieve their financial goals and create a steady stream of passive income through real estate rentals."

# Disclaimer

"The information provided in this book is for general informational purposes only and is not intended as legal, financial, or professional advice. The author and publisher make no representations or warranties, express or implied, as to the completeness, accuracy, reliability, or suitability of the information contained in this book. The author and publisher shall not be liable for any loss or damages, including without limitation, indirect or consequential loss or damage, arising from the use of the information in this book.

Investing in real estate rental properties carries a certain level of risk, and the strategies and best practices outlined in this book may not be suitable for every individual. It's important to consult with a financial advisor, a real estate attorney, and a tax professional before making any investment decisions. The author and publisher of this book do not endorse any specific investment strategies and readers are advised to conduct their own research and due diligence before making any investment decisions.

This book is not a substitute for professional advice and it's important to consult with a professional before taking any action based on the information provided in this book. The author and publisher do not take any responsibility for any errors or omissions in the information provided in this book."

# CHAPTERS          Page No.

Understanding the Potential of Real Estate Rentals for Financial Freedom    7

Finding the Right Properties: Strategies for Identifying and Acquiring Profitable Rental Properties    12

Maximizing Rental Income: Techniques for Setting RentPrices and Increasing Occupancy    26

Managing Rental Properties: Tips for Effective Property Management and Maintenance    79

Building a Rental Portfolio: Strategies for Expanding Your Rental Business and Increasing Income    119

Tax Advantages and Legal Considerations: Understanding the Tax and Legal Implications of Owning Rental Properties    145

Financing Your Rental Business: Options for Funding Your Rental Business and Managing Cash Flow    153

Conclusion: Achieving Financial Freedom through Real Estate Rentals - Tips, Trick and Best practices    165

# Chapter 1: Understanding the Potential of Real Estate Rentals for Financial Freedom

The concept of financial freedom is a desirable goal for many individuals, and real estate rentals can be a powerful tool for achieving that goal. This book, "Rent to Wealth: The Proven Path to Financial Freedom through Rental Property," is designed to provide readers with a comprehensive understanding of the potential of real estate rentals as a means of creating long-term wealth and financial freedom.

One of the primary benefits of real estate rentals is the ability to generate passive income. Unlike traditional forms of employment, rental properties can provide a steady stream of income without the need for active participation. This can allow individuals to achieve financial freedom and achieve their goals, such as retiring early or pursuing other endeavors.

Additionally, rental properties can appreciate in value over time, providing an additional source of wealth through capital gains. Furthermore, rental properties can also provide tax benefits, such as deductions for mortgage interest and depreciation.

However, it's important to note that, as with any investment, there are also risks associated with owning rental properties. Therefore, it's important to have a thorough understanding of the real estate market, property management, and the legal and financial aspects of owning rental properties before investing.

This book will provide readers with a step-by-step guide to understanding the potential of real estate rentals for financial freedom, including strategies for finding and acquiring profitable properties, maximizing rental income, managing properties, building a rental portfolio, and understanding the legal and financial considerations involved.

By the end of this book, readers will have the knowledge and tools they need to make informed decisions about investing in rental properties and creating a path to financial freedom through real estate rentals.

In addition to providing a steady stream of passive income and potential for appreciation, owning rental properties can also offer the potential for leverage. Leverage refers to using borrowed funds to increase the potential return on an investment. In the case of rental properties, leverage can be achieved by obtaining a mortgage to purchase a property, allowing the investor to own a property worth much more than the amount of cash invested. This can result in a higher potential return on investment, but it also increases the risk, as the investor is also responsible for repaying the mortgage.

Another advantage of rental properties is the opportunity to create long-term wealth. As rental properties appreciate in value over time, they can provide a significant source of wealth through capital gains. Additionally, rental properties can also provide a hedge against inflation, as rental prices tend to rise with inflation, allowing landlords to increase rent to keep up with the rising cost of living.

However, it's important to remember that owning rental properties is not a get-rich-quick scheme. It requires a significant amount of time, effort and resources to manage and maintain rental properties, and there are always risks involved. Therefore, it is important to thoroughly research the real estate market and have a clear understanding of the financial and legal considerations involved before investing.

This book will provide readers with a comprehensive understanding of the potential of real estate rentals for financial freedom, as well as the knowledge and tools they need to make informed decisions about investing in rental properties. It will cover strategies for finding and acquiring profitable properties, maximizing rental income, managing properties, building a rental portfolio, and understanding the legal and financial considerations involved. By following the strategies outlined in this book, readers will be able to create a path to financial freedom through real estate rentals.

Moreover, owning rental properties can also provide a sense of accomplishment and pride of ownership. Many people find it fulfilling to own a tangible asset that can provide a steady stream of income and appreciate in value over time. Additionally, owning rental properties can also provide a sense of control over one's financial future, as the income generated by the properties can be used to achieve financial goals such as saving for retirement or paying off debt.

However, it's important to remember that owning rental properties is not without its challenges. As a landlord, you will be responsible for finding and vetting tenants, collecting rent, maintaining and repairing the property, and dealing with any legal issues that may arise. It's important to have a clear understanding of the responsibilities involved and to be prepared to put in the time and effort required to effectively manage the properties.

Additionally, owning rental properties also requires a significant amount of capital, which can make it difficult for some individuals to get started. However, there are also alternative ways to invest in real estate, such as REITs, partnership and crowdfunding, these methods can provide a way for individuals to invest in real estate without having to own the property directly.

In this book, "Rent to Wealth: The Proven Path to Financial Freedom through Rental Property," we will explore all aspects of real estate rentals as a means of creating wealth and financial freedom. We will cover everything from finding and acquiring profitable properties, maximizing rental income, managing properties, building a rental portfolio, understanding the legal and financial considerations, and alternative ways to invest in real estate. By the end of this book, readers will have a complete understanding of how to create a path to financial freedom through real estate rentals.

*"Real estate rental is not a get-rich-quick scheme, but rather a powerful tool for building long-term wealth and achieving financial freedom"*

## Notes

..................................................................................

..................................................................................

..................................................................................

# Chapter 2: Finding the Right Properties: Strategies for Identifying and Acquiring Profitable Rental Properties

In order to make a profit from rental properties, it is crucial to find and acquire the right properties. This chapter will provide you with strategies for identifying and acquiring profitable rental properties.

The first step in finding the right properties is to research the market. You should research the different areas in which you are interested in investing, including information on the local economy, demographics, and the real estate market. This information will help you identify areas with strong rental demand, which will make it easier to find and acquire profitable properties.

Another key strategy is to focus on properties that are in good condition. Properties that are in need of repairs or renovations can be more costly and time-consuming to manage. Therefore, it is best to focus on properties that are move-in ready and have a low vacancy rate.

It's also important to consider the location of the property. Properties located in desirable areas, such as close to schools, transportation, and amenities, will be more attractive to renters and will likely have a higher rental rate.

Another strategy for identifying profitable properties is to look for properties that are undervalued. This can include properties that are being sold at a discount due to their condition or properties that are in an up-and-coming area.

You can also reach out to a real estate agent or property management company who can help you identify and acquire profitable rental properties. They can provide you with valuable information and resources, and can also help you negotiate the purchase price and handle the closing process.

It is also important to have a clear financial plan in place when acquiring rental properties. This includes understanding your budget, having enough cash reserves, and considering the potential cash flow, expenses, and return on investment before making an acquisition.

In conclusion, finding the right properties is crucial to the success of a rental property business. By researching the market, focusing on properties that are in good condition, considering location, looking for undervalued properties, and working with professionals, you can increase your chances of acquiring profitable rental properties.

Another strategy for finding profitable properties is networking and building relationships. This can include networking with other real estate investors, real estate agents, and property management companies. They can provide valuable insights and information on properties that may not be listed publicly and may be available at a discounted price. Joining a local real estate investing group or attending real estate investing events can also be a great way to expand your network and find potential properties.

It's also important to consider the rental property's cash flow, which is the amount of money left after all expenses are paid. A property with a positive cash flow will generate more income than expenses, while a property with a negative cash flow will generate less income than expenses. It's important to consider the potential cash flow when evaluating properties, as a property with a positive cash flow can generate a steady stream of income and will be easier to maintain in the long run.

Another important factor to consider when evaluating properties is the potential for appreciation. This refers to the increase in value of the property over time. Properties located in areas with strong economic growth and development are more likely to appreciate in value, which can provide a significant source of wealth through capital gains.

It's also important to have a clear understanding of the legal and financial considerations involved in acquiring rental properties. This can include understanding the process of buying a property, familiarizing yourself with local zoning laws, and having a clear understanding of the tax implications of owning rental properties. It is a good idea to consult with a real estate attorney or accountant before acquiring any properties.

In summary, finding the right properties is crucial to the success of a rental property business. By researching the market, focusing on properties that are in good condition, considering location, looking for undervalued properties, networking and building relationships, having a clear financial plan, and understanding the legal and financial considerations, you can increase your chances of acquiring profitable rental properties.

Another important factor to consider when evaluating rental properties is the rental demand in the area. Properties located in areas with high rental demand will be more likely to be occupied and generate a steady stream of income. You can research the rental demand in an area by looking at the vacancy rates, rental prices, and the number of properties available for rent.

It's also important to consider the type of property you want to invest in. Single-family homes, duplexes, and small apartment buildings are all options, but each has its own set of pros and cons. Single-family homes are usually easier to manage, but they may be more expensive to purchase and maintain. Duplexes and small apartment buildings can generate a higher income, but they may also require more management and maintenance. It's important to consider your own skills, resources, and goals when choosing the type of property to invest in.

Another strategy for finding profitable rental properties is to look for properties that are being sold by motivated sellers. These are individuals who are eager to sell their property quickly, such as those who are facing foreclosure, going through a divorce, or relocating. These properties can be purchased at a discounted price, which can increase the potential for profit.

Finally, it's important to have a plan in place for managing the properties once they are acquired. This includes having a clear understanding of the responsibilities involved in property management, creating a budget, and having a plan in place for finding and vetting tenants, collecting rent, and handling maintenance and repairs. It's also important to have a system in place for tracking income and expenses to ensure the properties are generating a positive cash flow.

In summary, finding the right properties is crucial to the success of a rental property business. By researching the market, focusing on properties that are in good condition, considering location, looking for undervalued properties, networking and building relationships, having a clear financial plan, understanding the legal and financial considerations, considering rental demand and type of property, finding motivated sellers and having a plan for managing properties, you can increase your chances of acquiring profitable rental properties.

Another key strategy for finding profitable rental properties is to look for properties that have potential for adding value. This can include properties that are in need of some cosmetic repairs or renovations, or properties that have potential for adding additional living space, such as a basement or attic. By investing in these types of properties, you can potentially increase the rental income and the property value.

It's also important to consider the long-term prospects of the area you are investing in. Properties located in areas with strong economic growth, good schools and infrastructure, and a growing population are more likely to appreciate in value and generate a steady stream of rental income over the long-term.

You can also consider looking for properties that have a unique selling point. This can include properties that have a unique architectural design, are located in a historic district, or have a unique feature such as a large backyard or a swimming pool. These properties can be more attractive to renters and can command a higher rent.

Another strategy for finding profitable rental properties is to look for properties that are being sold by financial institutions such as banks and government agencies. These properties are usually priced lower than market value, and can be a great opportunity for investors to acquire properties at a discounted price.

Additionally, you can also consider looking for properties that are being sold at auction. These properties are usually sold at a discounted price, and can be a great opportunity for investors to acquire properties at a lower cost.

In conclusion, finding the right properties is crucial to the success of a rental property business. By researching the market, focusing on properties that are in good condition, considering location, looking for undervalued properties, networking and building relationships, having a clear financial plan, understanding the legal and financial considerations, considering rental demand and type of property, finding motivated sellers, adding value, looking for long-term prospects, unique selling points, financial institutions and auction properties, and having a plan for managing properties, you can increase your chances of acquiring profitable rental properties.

Another strategy for finding profitable rental properties is to look for properties that have multiple income streams. For example, properties that have a separate basement or garage that can be rented out as a separate unit can provide additional income. Another example is a property that has a large backyard that can be used for gardening or farming, which can be rented out to local farmers or community gardens. This can provide additional income and also make the property more attractive to renters.

You can also consider looking for properties that are part of a government-funded program. For example, the Low-Income Housing Tax Credit (LIHTC) program provides tax credits to developers who build or rehabilitate affordable rental housing for low-income households. Investing in properties that are part of this program can provide a steady stream of income and can also provide a sense of social responsibility.

Another strategy for finding profitable rental properties is to look for properties that have been recently built or renovated. For example, properties that are Energy Star certified or have other energy-efficient features can help to lower utility costs and make the property more attractive to renters. Additionally, properties that have been recently built or renovated are more likely to be in good condition, which can reduce the cost of maintenance and repairs.

Finally, you can also consider looking for properties that are being sold by the government, such as HUD homes or VA foreclosures. These properties are usually priced lower than market value, and can be a great opportunity for investors to acquire properties at a discounted price.

In summary, finding the right properties is crucial to the success of a rental property business. By researching the market, focusing on properties that are in good condition, considering location, looking for undervalued properties, networking and building relationships, having a clear financial plan, understanding the legal and financial considerations, considering rental demand and type of property, finding motivated sellers, adding value, looking for long-term prospects, unique selling points, financial institutions and auction properties, government funded programs, recently built or renovated properties and government-owned properties, and having a plan for managing properties, you can increase your chances of acquiring profitable rental properties.

Another strategy for finding profitable rental properties is to look for properties that have been recently foreclosed or short-sold. These properties are often sold at a discounted price and can be a great opportunity for investors to acquire properties at a lower cost. However, it's important to thoroughly research the condition of the property and any potential legal issues before making an offer, as these properties may have been vacant for an extended period of time, and may have issues such as mold or structural damage.

You can also consider looking for properties that have been previously owned by landlords or real estate investors. These properties are more likely to have been well-maintained and may have been updated with features such as new appliances or flooring. Additionally, these properties may have existing tenants and a history of rental income, which can provide valuable information on the potential cash flow and rental income of the property.

Another strategy for finding profitable rental properties is to look for properties that are being sold by owner. These properties are often sold at a discounted price, as the owner is not paying commissions to a real estate agent, which can make them a great opportunity for investors to acquire properties at a lower cost. However, it's important to thoroughly research the condition of the property and any potential legal issues before making an offer.

Finally, you can also consider looking for properties that are being sold at a bulk discount. For example, a real estate investor may be looking to sell several properties at once and may be willing to sell them at a discounted price. This can be a great opportunity for investors to acquire multiple properties at a lower cost and build a rental portfolio quickly.

In summary, finding the right properties is crucial to the success of a rental property business. By researching the market, focusing on properties that are in good condition, considering location, looking for undervalued properties, networking and building relationships, having a clear financial plan, understanding the legal and financial considerations, considering rental demand and type of property, finding motivated sellers, adding value, looking for long-term prospects, unique selling points, financial institutions and auction properties, government funded programs, recently built or renovated properties.

In conclusion, finding the right properties is crucial to the success of a rental property business. By researching the market, focusing on properties that are in good condition, considering location, looking for undervalued properties, networking and building relationships, having a clear financial plan, understanding the legal and financial considerations, considering rental demand and type of property, finding motivated sellers, adding value, looking for long-term prospects, unique selling points, financial institutions, auction properties, government-funded programs, recently built or renovated properties, government-owned properties, foreclosed or short-sold properties, previously owned by landlords or real estate investors, owner-sold properties, and bulk discounted properties, you can increase your chances of acquiring profitable rental properties. This chapter has provided you with the strategies and information needed to identify and acquire the right properties for your rental property business. It is important to keep in mind that finding the right properties is just one step in the process of building a successful rental property business, and it is crucial to continue to research and educate yourself on the other aspects of the business such as managing and maintaining properties, renting and legal considerations.

*"The art of finding the right rental properties is not in discovering the perfect properties, but in finding the properties that can be made perfect"*

Another important aspect of finding the right properties is being aware of current market trends and conditions. This includes keeping an eye on the interest rates, inflation, and the overall state of the economy, as these factors can affect the real estate market and have a direct impact on your rental properties. For example, during times of economic recession, the rental demand may decrease, and it may be harder to find tenants, whereas during times of economic growth, the rental demand may increase and it will be easier to find tenants.

Furthermore, it's important to be aware of the type of tenants you want to attract, and to look for properties that will appeal to them. For example, if you are targeting families, you may want to look for properties that are located near good schools and have a backyard. If you are targeting students, you may want to look for properties that are located near universities and have multiple bedrooms. Understanding your target market and looking for properties that will appeal to them can help increase your chances of finding tenants and generating income.

Additionally, it's important to have a clear understanding of your investment goals and to align them with the properties you are considering. For example, if you are looking for short-term investments, you may want to look for properties that are in high-demand areas with a high rental yield. If you are looking for long-term investments, you may want to look for properties that have potential for appreciation and have a lower rental yield but have a higher potential for capital gains.

In conclusion, finding the right properties is a crucial aspect of building a successful rental property business. By researching the market, focusing on properties that are in good condition, considering location, looking for undervalued properties, networking and building relationships, having a clear financial plan, understanding the legal and financial considerations, considering rental demand and type of property, finding motivated sellers, adding value, looking for long-term prospects, unique selling points, financial institutions, auction properties, government-funded programs, recently built or renovated properties, government-owned properties, foreclosed or short-sold properties, previously owned by landlords or real estate investors, owner-sold properties, and bulk discounted properties, you can increase your chances of acquiring profitable rental properties.

Additionally, it's important to be aware of current market trends and conditions, understand your target tenant market, and have a clear understanding of your investment goals in order to make informed decisions when finding the right properties for your rental property business.

*"In Finding the Right Properties, learn strategies for identifying profitable rental properties that align with your goals and long-term strategy"*

## Notes

..................................................................................................

..................................................................................................

..................................................................................................

# Chapter 3: Maximizing Rental Income: Techniques for Setting Rent Prices and Increasing Occupancy

One of the most important factors in creating a successful rental property business is maximizing rental income. This includes setting the right rent prices and increasing occupancy. In this chapter, we will discuss various techniques for setting rent prices and increasing occupancy to help you maximize your rental income.

Setting the right rent price is crucial to ensuring that your property is competitive in the market and attracting tenants. One technique for setting rent prices is to research the market and compare the rent prices of similar properties in the area. This can give you an idea of what the going rate is for similar properties and help you set a competitive rent price. It's also important to consider the condition of your property, any upgrades or renovations that have been made, and the location when setting rent prices.

Another technique for setting rent prices is to conduct a rental evaluation. This is a process that involves assessing the condition of the property, the local market conditions, and the property's amenities to determine the optimal rent price. A rental evaluation can also take into account any potential upgrades or renovations that may be necessary to increase the property's value and rental income.

Increasing occupancy is another key factor in maximizing rental income. One technique for increasing occupancy is to create an attractive listing for the property. This includes taking high-quality photos and providing a detailed description of the property, including its location, amenities, and any upgrades or renovations that have been made. By creating an attractive listing, you can increase the chances of attracting potential tenants.

Another technique for increasing occupancy is to offer incentives to tenants. This can include offering a discount on the first month's rent, including utilities in the rent, or offering a flexible lease option. By offering incentives, you can increase the chances of attracting tenants and filling vacancies quickly.

Another way to increase the occupancy rate is to improve the property's amenities, for example by adding a pool, gym, or a rooftop terrace. By providing additional amenities, you can make your property more attractive to potential tenants and increase its value.

Finally, providing good customer service and responsive maintenance can also increase the occupancy rate. By responding quickly to tenant concerns, providing regular maintenance and keeping the property in good condition, you can attract and retain tenants.

In conclusion, maximizing rental income is crucial to the success of a rental property business. By setting the right rent prices, conducting rental evaluations, creating an attractive listing, offering incentives, improving amenities and providing good customer service and responsive maintenance, you can increase the chances of filling vacancies and maximizing your rental income.

Another technique for increasing occupancy is to establish a strong online presence. This includes having a professional website, creating social media accounts, and advertising the property on online rental platforms such as Zillow, Trulia, and Craigslist. By having a strong online presence, you can reach a larger audience and increase the chances of attracting potential tenants.

You can also consider offering flexible lease options to potential tenants. For example, offering short-term leases or month-to-month leases can attract a wider range of tenants, including students, business travelers, and those who are relocating temporarily. This can help to fill vacancies more quickly and increase the overall occupancy rate.

Another technique for increasing occupancy is to offer furnished properties. By providing furniture and household appliances, you can make the property more attractive to potential tenants and increase the chances of filling vacancies. This can be especially beneficial for properties located near universities or business centers, as it can attract students or business travelers who are looking for a temporary place to stay.

Additionally, it's important to have a good marketing strategy in place to reach potential tenants. This can include traditional marketing methods such as print ads, billboards, or flyers, as well as digital marketing methods such as email marketing, pay-per-click advertising, and social media advertising. By having a good marketing strategy in place, you can reach a larger audience and increase the chances of filling vacancies.

Lastly, you can also consider offering added value services to tenants. For example, offering a concierge service, housekeeping, or laundry services can make the property more attractive to potential tenants and increase the chances of filling vacancies. This can also increase the rental income as tenants may be willing to pay a premium for these services.

In conclusion, maximizing rental income is crucial to the success of a rental property business. By setting the right rent prices, conducting rental evaluations, creating an attractive listing, offering incentives, improving amenities, providing good customer service and responsive maintenance, establish a strong online presence, offering flexible lease options, offering furnished properties, having a good marketing strategy and offering added value services, you can increase the chances of filling vacancies and maximizing your rental income.

Another technique for increasing occupancy is to establish a good reputation as a landlord. This includes being responsive to tenant needs, providing good customer service, and being fair and consistent when dealing with tenants. By establishing a good reputation, you can attract and retain tenants, and increase the chances of filling vacancies. Positive word-of-mouth and online reviews can be an important factor in attracting new tenants.

You can also consider offering a loyalty program for long-term tenants. For example, offering a rent discount for tenants who renew their lease or a referral program for tenants who bring in new renters can help retain current tenants and fill vacancies more quickly.

Another way to increase occupancy is to make the rental application process as easy and streamlined as possible. This can include offering online applications and digital signature capabilities, as well as having a clear and transparent screening process. By making the rental application process easy and convenient, you can attract more potential tenants and increase the chances of filling vacancies.

You can also consider offering a pet-friendly policy. Many renters own pets, and by allowing pets in your rental properties, you can increase the pool of potential tenants and reduce the chances of vacancies. However, it's important to have a clear policy in place and to charge a pet deposit or pet fee to mitigate any potential damage caused by pets.

Finally, being proactive in managing and maintaining the property can also help increase occupancy. This includes regular maintenance, such as cleaning common areas, maintaining the landscaping, and addressing any repairs or upgrades needed. By keeping the property in good condition, you can attract and retain tenants, and increase the overall occupancy rate.

In conclusion, maximizing rental income is crucial to the success of a rental property business. By setting the right rent prices, conducting rental evaluations, creating an attractive listing, offering incentives, improving amenities, providing good customer service, being responsive to tenant needs, being fair and consistent with tenants, establish a strong online presence, offering flexible lease options, offering furnished properties, having a good marketing strategy, offering added value services, establishing a good reputation, offering loyalty program, making the rental application process easy, offering a pet-friendly policy, and being proactive in managing and maintaining the property, you can increase the chances of filling vacancies and maximizing your rental income.

Another way to increase occupancy is to offer flexible lease terms. This can include offering month-to-month or short-term leases, which can be attractive to renters who are looking for a more temporary or flexible living arrangement. Offering flexible lease terms can also help fill vacancies more quickly, as it can appeal to a wider range of renters.

You can also consider offering bundled services, such as internet, cable, or utilities. By including these services in the rent, you can make the property more attractive to potential tenants and increase the chances of filling vacancies. Additionally, offering bundled services can also help to reduce the number of bills that tenants have to pay, which can be a positive selling point.

You can also consider offering move-in specials or discounts to attract tenants. For example, offering a discount on the first month's rent or including a free parking spot can be an attractive incentive for potential tenants.

Lastly, it's important to have a good understanding of the legal aspects of being a landlord. This includes being familiar with the Fair Housing Act, understanding the eviction process, and being aware of the state and local laws regarding rental properties. By having a good understanding of the legal aspects of being a landlord, you can ensure that you are in compliance with all laws and regulations and avoid any potential legal issues.

In conclusion, maximizing rental income is crucial to the success of a rental property business. By setting the right rent prices, conducting rental evaluations, creating an attractive listing, offering incentives, improving amenities, providing good customer service, being responsive to tenant needs, being fair and consistent with tenants, establish a strong online presence, offering flexible lease options, offering flexible lease terms, offering bundled services, move-in specials or discounts, and having a good understanding of the legal aspects of being a landlord, you can increase the chances of filling vacancies and maximizing your rental income. By using these techniques, you can optimize your rental income and create a thriving rental property business.

Another technique for increasing occupancy is to establish a good relationship with your tenants. This can include regular communication, being responsive to their needs, and being willing to listen to feedback and make improvements to the property. By building a good relationship with your tenants, you can increase the chances of renewing leases and attract new tenants through positive word-of-mouth.

You can also consider offering a rewards program for on-time rent payments. This can include offering a small discount on the rent or a gift card. This can encourage tenants to pay their rent on time and can help to reduce the number of late payments.

Another way to increase occupancy is to make the property as energy-efficient as possible. This can include installing energy-efficient appliances, adding insulation, or upgrading to energy-efficient lighting. By making the property more energy-efficient, you can reduce the utility costs for the tenants, which can be an attractive selling point and also reduce the environmental impact.

Lastly, you can also consider offering virtual tours or virtual open houses to potential tenants. By offering virtual tours, you can reach a larger audience and increase the chances of filling vacancies, as potential tenants can view the property from the comfort of their own home. Additionally, virtual tours can also help to reduce the number of in-person showings, which can be beneficial during times of social distancing.

In conclusion, maximizing rental income is crucial to the success of a rental property business. By setting the right rent prices, conducting rental evaluations, creating an attractive listing, offering incentives, improving amenities, providing good customer service, being responsive to tenant needs, being fair and consistent with tenants, establish a strong online presence, offering flexible lease options, offering flexible lease terms, offering bundled services, move-in specials or discounts, having a good understanding of the legal aspects of being a landlord, establishing a good relationship with your tenants, offering a rewards program, making the property energy-efficient, and offering virtual tours, you can increase the chances of filling vacancies and maximizing your rental income.

Another technique for increasing occupancy is to offer special promotions or events to attract tenants. This can include offering a move-in special, hosting an open house, or organizing a tenant appreciation event. By offering special promotions or events, you can increase the chances of filling vacancies and creating a positive image for your property.

You can also consider offering additional services to your tenants. For example, offering a concierge service or a package receiving service can make your property more attractive to potential tenants and increase the chances of filling vacancies. Additionally, offering additional services can also increase the rental income, as tenants may be willing to pay a premium for these services.

Another way to increase occupancy is to have a good understanding of the local market conditions. This includes being aware of the supply and demand, population trends, and any upcoming development projects. By having a good understanding of the local market conditions, you can make informed decisions about the rental prices and the type of properties that are in demand.

Finally, you can also consider offering a flexible payment option for the rent. This can include offering the option to pay rent online or by automatic bank transfer, which can be convenient for tenants and can also reduce the number of late payments.

In conclusion, maximizing rental income is crucial to the success of a rental property business. By setting the right rent prices, conducting rental evaluations, creating an attractive listing, offering incentives, improving amenities, providing good customer service, being responsive to tenant needs, being fair and consistent with tenants, establish a strong online presence, offering flexible lease options, offering flexible lease terms, offering bundled services, move-in specials or discounts, having a good understanding of the legal aspects of being a landlord, establishing a good relationship with your tenants, offering a rewards program, making the property energy-efficient, offering virtual tours, offering special promotions or events, offering additional services, having a good understanding of the local market conditions and offering a flexible payment option, you can increase the chances of filling vacancies and maximizing your rental income.

Another technique for increasing occupancy is to have a flexible move-in policy. This can include offering flexible move-in dates, allowing tenants to move in on weekends, and being willing to work with tenants who have unique move-in schedules. By having a flexible move-in policy, you can increase the chances of filling vacancies and attract tenants who have a tight move-in schedule.

You can also consider offering added security features to your properties. This can include installing security cameras, adding keyless entry systems, or offering a security guard service. By offering added security features, you can make your property more attractive to potential tenants and increase the chances of filling vacancies.

Another way to increase occupancy is to have a good understanding of the local economy. This includes being aware of the employment rate, the local economy growth, and the median income of the area. By having a good understanding of the local economy, you can make informed decisions about the rental prices and the type of properties that are in demand.

Finally, you can also consider offering a flexible payment option for the security deposit. This can include offering the option to pay the security deposit in multiple installments or by automatic bank transfer. This can be convenient for tenants and can also help to reduce the number of late payments.

In conclusion, maximizing rental income is crucial to the success of a rental property business. By setting the right rent prices, conducting rental evaluations, creating an attractive listing, offering incentives, improving amenities, providing good customer service, being responsive to tenant needs, being fair and consistent with tenants, establish a strong online presence, offering flexible lease options, offering flexible lease terms, offering bundled services, move-in specials or discounts, having a good understanding of the legal aspects of being a landlord, establishing a good relationship with your tenants, offering a rewards program, making the property energy-efficient, offering virtual tours, offering special promotions or events, offering additional services, having a good understanding of the local market conditions, offering a flexible payment option, having a flexible move-in policy, offering added security features, having a good understanding of the local economy, and offering a flexible payment option for the security deposit, you can increase the chances of filling vacancies and maximizing your rental income.

Another technique for increasing occupancy is to offer a renter's insurance program. By requiring tenants to have renter's insurance, you can provide added protection for your property and also ensure that tenants are covered in case of any accidents or damages. This can make your property more attractive to potential tenants and increase the chances of filling vacancies.

You can also consider offering a tenant portal, where tenants can access their lease agreement, pay rent, request maintenance, and communicate with you. By offering a tenant portal, you can make it easy for tenants to manage their rental experience and increase the chances of filling vacancies.

Another way to increase occupancy is to have a good understanding of the local transportation. This includes being aware of the public transportation options, proximity to major highways, and any upcoming transportation projects. By having a good understanding of the local transportation, you can make informed decisions about the rental prices and the type of properties that are in demand.

Finally, you can also consider offering a flexible payment option for the utilities. This can include offering the option to pay the utilities in multiple installments or by automatic bank transfer. This can be convenient for tenants and can also help to reduce the number of late payments.

In conclusion, maximizing rental income is crucial to the success of a rental property business. By setting the right rent prices, conducting rental evaluations, creating an attractive listing, offering incentives, improving amenities, providing good customer service, being responsive to tenant needs, being fair and consistent with tenants, establish a strong online presence, offering flexible lease options, offering flexible lease terms, offering bundled services, move-in specials or discounts, having a good understanding of the legal aspects of being a landlord, establishing a good relationship with your tenants, offering a rewards program, making the property energy-efficient, offering virtual tours, offering special promotions or events, offering additional services, having a good understanding of the local market conditions, offering a flexible payment option, having a flexible move-in policy, offering added security features, having a good understanding of the local economy, offering a flexible payment option for the security deposit, offering a renter's insurance program, offering a tenant portal, having a good understanding of the local transportation and offering a flexible payment option for the utilities, you can increase the chances of filling vacancies and maximizing your rental income.

Another technique for increasing occupancy is to offer a rent-to-own option. By offering a rent-to-own option, you can attract renters who are looking to eventually purchase a property and increase the chances of filling vacancies. This can also provide an incentive for tenants to take good care of the property, as they have the potential to purchase it in the future.

You can also consider offering a community space or amenities. This can include a community garden, a shared workspace, or a community pool. By offering a community space or amenities, you can make your property more attractive to potential tenants and increase the chances of filling vacancies.

Another way to increase occupancy is to have a good understanding of the local demographics. This includes being aware of the age range, income level, and family size of the area. By having a good understanding of the local demographics, you can make informed decisions about the rental prices and the type of properties that are in demand.

Finally, you can also consider offering a flexible payment option for parking. This can include offering the option to pay for parking in multiple installments or by automatic bank transfer. This can be convenient for tenants and can also help to reduce the number of late payments.

In conclusion, maximizing rental income is crucial to the success of a rental property business. By setting the right rent prices, conducting rental evaluations, creating an attractive listing, offering incentives, improving amenities, providing good customer service, being responsive to tenant needs, being fair and consistent with tenants, establish a strong online presence, offering flexible lease options, offering flexible lease terms, offering bundled services, move-in specials or discounts, having a good understanding of the legal aspects of being a landlord, establishing a good relationship with your tenants, offering a rewards program, making the property energy-efficient, offering virtual tours, offering special promotions or events, offering additional services, having a good understanding of the local market conditions, offering a flexible payment option, having a flexible move-in policy, offering added security features, having a good understanding of the local economy, offering a flexible payment option for the security deposit, offering a renter's insurance program, offering a tenant portal, having a good understanding of the local transportation, offering a flexible payment option for the utilities, offering a rent-to-own option, offering a community space or amenities, and having a good understanding of the local demographics, you can increase the chances of filling vacancies and maximizing your rental income. Additionally, by offering a flexible payment option for parking, you can provide an added convenience for tenants and increase occupancy. Overall, by using a combination of these techniques, you can create a successful rental property business that provides a steady stream of rental income and the potential for long-term financial freedom.

Another technique for increasing occupancy is to offer a pet-friendly policy. By allowing tenants to have pets, you can attract renters who have pets and increase the chances of filling vacancies. However, it's important to have clear guidelines and regulations in place, such as size and breed restrictions, and a pet deposit or monthly pet fee to ensure that the property is well-maintained and protected.

You can also consider offering a maintenance and repair service. By having a dedicated maintenance and repair team, you can respond quickly to tenants' requests and ensure that the property is always in good condition. This can also increase the chances of tenants renewing their leases and attract new tenants.

Another way to increase occupancy is to have a good understanding of the local amenities. This includes being aware of the local schools, parks, shopping centers, and other amenities. By having a good understanding of the local amenities, you can make informed decisions about the rental prices and the type of properties that are in demand.

Finally, you can also consider offering a loyalty program for long-term tenants. This can include offering a rent discount or other incentives for tenants who have been renting for a certain period of time. This can encourage tenants to stay longer and increase occupancy.

In conclusion, maximizing rental income is crucial to the success of a rental property business. By setting the right rent prices, conducting rental evaluations, creating an attractive listing, offering incentives, improving amenities, providing good customer service, being responsive to tenant needs, being fair and consistent with tenants, establish a strong online presence, offering flexible lease options, offering flexible lease terms, offering bundled services, move-in specials or discounts, having a good understanding of the legal aspects of being a landlord, establishing a good relationship with your tenants, offering a rewards program, making the property energy-efficient, offering virtual tours, offering special promotions or events, offering additional services, having a good understanding of the local market conditions, offering a flexible payment option, having a flexible move-in policy, offering added security features, having a good understanding of the local economy, offering a flexible payment option for the security deposit, offering a renter's insurance program, offering a tenant portal, having a good understanding of the local transportation, offering a flexible payment option for the utilities, offering a rent-to-own option, offering a community space or amenities, having a good understanding of the local demographics, offering a pet-friendly policy, offering a maintenance and repair service, having a good understanding of the local amenities and offering a loyalty program for long-term tenants, you can increase the chances of filling vacancies and maximizing your rental income.

Another technique for increasing occupancy is to offer furnished or semi-furnished options. By offering furnished or semi-furnished options, you can make your property more attractive to potential tenants, especially those who are looking for a short-term rental or are relocating to the area. Additionally, you can also charge a premium for these options, which can increase your rental income.

You can also consider offering a referral program for new tenants. By offering a referral program, you can incentivize current tenants to refer their friends and family to your property. This can help to increase occupancy and also attract high-quality tenants.

Another way to increase occupancy is to have a good understanding of the local rental market. This includes being aware of the average rental prices, the types of properties that are in demand, and any upcoming developments or trends. By having a good understanding of the local rental market, you can make informed decisions about the rental prices and the type of properties that are in demand.

Finally, you can also consider offering a flexible lease option, such as a month-to-month lease. By offering a flexible lease option, you can attract renters who are looking for short-term rentals or are unsure of their long-term plans. Additionally, a flexible lease option can also help to increase occupancy and reduce the chances of vacancies.

In conclusion, maximizing rental income is crucial to the success of a rental property business. By setting the right rent prices, conducting rental evaluations, creating an attractive listing, offering incentives, improving amenities, providing good customer service, being responsive to tenant needs, being fair and consistent with tenants, establish a strong online presence, offering flexible lease options, offering flexible lease terms, offering bundled services, move-in specials or discounts, having a good understanding of the legal aspects of being a landlord, establishing a good relationship with your tenants, offering a rewards program, making the property energy-efficient, offering virtual tours, offering special promotions or events, offering additional services, having a good understanding of the local market conditions, offering a flexible payment option, having a flexible move-in policy, offering added security features, having a good understanding of the local economy, offering a flexible payment option for the security deposit, offering a renter's insurance program, offering a tenant portal, having a good understanding of the local transportation, offering a flexible payment option for the utilities, offering a rent-to-own option, offering a community space or amenities, having a good understanding of the local demographics, offering a pet-friendly policy, offering a maintenance and repair service, having a good understanding of the local amenities, offering a loyalty program for long-term tenants, offering furnished or semi-furnished options, offering a referral program for new tenants, having a good understanding of the local rental market, and offering a flexible lease option, you can increase the chances of filling vacancies and maximizing your rental income.

Another strategy to consider is implementing smart home technology in your rental properties. By offering features such as keyless entry, remote temperature control, and energy monitoring, you can attract tech-savvy renters and increase the appeal of your properties.

Another important aspect to consider is providing exceptional customer service. By being responsive to tenant requests, addressing issues promptly, and going above and beyond to meet their needs, you can create positive relationships with your tenants and increase the likelihood of them renewing their leases or referring others to your properties.

Finally, it's also important to stay up to date with the legal requirements and regulations for being a landlord. This includes understanding fair housing laws, eviction procedures, and other legal matters that may arise. By staying informed and compliant, you can minimize legal issues and protect your rental income.

In conclusion, there are many strategies that can be used to maximize rental income and fill vacancies. By implementing a combination of these techniques and constantly evaluating and adapting your approach, you can create a successful rental property business that provides a steady stream of rental income and the potential for long-term financial freedom.

Another strategy to consider is implementing a property management software. By using a property management software, you can streamline your rental business and make it more efficient. The software can help you keep track of tenant information, rent payments, maintenance requests, and other important details. This can help you stay organized and make it easier to manage your properties.

Another important aspect to consider is staying involved with the local rental community. This includes networking with other landlords, joining a local landlord association, and staying informed about local events and trends. By staying connected with other landlords, you can gain valuable insights and knowledge about the rental market, and stay informed about any changes or new opportunities in the area.

Additionally, it's also important to be proactive in marketing your properties. This can include creating an attractive listing with high-quality photos and videos, promoting your properties on social media and online listing sites, and advertising in local newspapers and classifieds. By actively marketing your properties, you can increase visibility and attract potential tenants.

Finally, it's also important to stay up-to-date with the latest trends and technologies in the rental industry. This includes being aware of new technologies such as virtual tours, online leasing and rent payments, and other innovations that can make your rental business more efficient and successful. By staying informed and adapting to new technologies, you can stay ahead of the competition and improve your rental income.

In conclusion, there are many strategies that can be used to maximize rental income and fill vacancies. By implementing a combination of these techniques and constantly evaluating and adapting your approach, you can create a successful rental property business that provides a steady stream of rental income and the potential for long-term financial freedom. By using property management software, staying involved with the local rental community, being proactive in marketing your properties, and staying up-to-date with the latest trends and technologies, you can optimize your rental income and achieve your financial goals.

Another strategy that can help to maximize rental income is to focus on building a strong online presence. This can include creating a professional website for your rental properties, managing online reviews, and creating engaging social media content. By building a strong online presence, you can reach a wider audience and attract potential tenants who are searching for rental properties online.

Another important aspect to consider is providing added value to your tenants. This can include offering free Wi-Fi, cable, or other amenities, such as a gym or pool. By providing added value to your tenants, you can make your properties more attractive and increase the chances of tenants renewing their leases.

Additionally, it's also important to be responsive to your tenants' needs. This can include addressing maintenance requests, responding to questions and concerns, and being available to communicate with your tenants. By being responsive, you can build trust and create positive relationships with your tenants, which can increase the chances of them renewing their leases.

Finally, it's also important to stay up-to-date with local laws and regulations. This includes understanding fair housing laws, eviction procedures, and any other legal requirements that may apply to your rental properties. By staying informed and compliant, you can minimize legal issues and protect your rental income.

In conclusion, there are many strategies that can be used to maximize rental income and fill vacancies. By implementing a combination of these techniques and constantly evaluating and adapting your approach, you can create a successful rental property business that provides a steady stream of rental income and the potential for long-term financial freedom. By building a strong online presence, providing added value to your tenants, being responsive to your tenants' needs, and staying up-to-date with local laws and regulations, you can optimize your rental income and achieve your financial goals.

Another strategy to consider is focusing on building a positive reputation in your community. This can include participating in local events, supporting local charities, and being a responsible and respectful landlord. By building a positive reputation in your community, you can attract potential tenants who are looking for a responsible and respectful landlord.

Another important aspect to consider is providing excellent customer service. This can include providing an easy and efficient process for move-in and move-out, handling maintenance requests promptly, and providing regular communication with your tenants. By providing excellent customer service, you can build trust and create positive relationships with your tenants, which can increase the chances of them renewing their leases.

Another way to increase occupancy is to have a good understanding of the local housing market. This includes being aware of the housing prices, the types of properties that are in demand, and any upcoming developments or trends. By having a good understanding of the local housing market, you can make informed decisions about the rental prices and the type of properties that are in demand.

Additionally, it is also important to have a flexible approach to your rental properties. This can include being open to different types of tenants, such as students, families, or professionals, and offering different types of lease agreements, such as month-to-month or long-term leases. By having a flexible approach, you can increase the chances of filling vacancies and maximizing your rental income.

In conclusion, there are many strategies that can be used to maximize rental income and fill vacancies. By implementing a combination of these techniques and constantly evaluating and adapting your approach, you can create a successful rental property business that provides a steady stream of rental income and the potential for long-term financial freedom. By focusing on building a positive reputation in your community, providing excellent customer service, having a good understanding of the local housing market, and having a flexible approach to your rental properties, you can optimize your rental income and achieve your financial goals.

Another strategy that can help to maximize rental income is to focus on energy efficiency in your properties. This can include installing energy-efficient appliances, providing insulation and weatherproofing, and promoting the use of renewable energy sources. By making your properties energy-efficient, you can lower your operating costs, attract environmentally-conscious tenants, and increase the appeal of your properties.

Another important aspect to consider is providing a good move-in experience. This can include providing a detailed walk-through of the property, giving new tenants information on how to use appliances and fixtures, and providing a checklist of items that need to be done before move-in. By providing a good move-in experience, you can set a positive tone for the tenancy and increase the chances of tenants renewing their leases.

Additionally, it's also important to have a good understanding of the local rental laws and regulations. This includes understanding fair housing laws, eviction procedures, and any other legal requirements that may apply to your rental properties. By staying informed and compliant, you can minimize legal issues and protect your rental income.

Finally, it's also important to stay up-to-date with the latest trends and technologies in the rental industry. This includes being aware of new technologies such as virtual tours, online leasing and rent payments, and other innovations that can make your rental business more efficient and successful. By staying informed and adapting to new technologies, you can stay ahead of the competition and improve your rental income.

In conclusion, there are many strategies that can be used to maximize rental income and fill vacancies. By implementing a combination of these techniques and constantly evaluating and adapting your approach, you can create a successful rental property business that provides a steady stream of rental income and the potential for long-term financial freedom. By focusing on energy efficiency, providing a good move-in experience, having a good understanding of the local rental laws and regulations, and staying up-to-date with the latest trends and technologies in the rental industry, you can optimize your rental income and achieve your financial goals.

Another strategy that can help to maximize rental income is to focus on maintenance and upkeep of your properties. This can include regular inspections, preventative maintenance, and timely repairs. By keeping your properties well-maintained, you can attract high-quality tenants, increase the appeal of your properties, and extend the life of your properties.

Another important aspect to consider is offering incentives to tenants. This can include discounts on rent, waived application fees, or other perks. By offering incentives, you can attract potential tenants and increase the chances of filling vacancies.

Additionally, it's also important to have a good understanding of the local rental market and economy. This includes being aware of the average rental prices, the types of properties that are in demand, and any upcoming developments or trends. By having a good understanding of the local rental market and economy, you can make informed decisions about the rental prices and the type of properties that are in demand.

Finally, it's also important to build a good relationship with your tenants. This can include regularly communicating with them, being responsive to their needs, and being fair and consistent in your dealings with them. By building a good relationship with your tenants, you can increase the chances of them renewing their leases and referring others to your properties.

In conclusion, there are many strategies that can be used to maximize rental income and fill vacancies. By implementing a combination of these techniques and constantly evaluating and adapting your approach, you can create a successful rental property business that provides a steady stream of rental income and the potential for long-term financial freedom. By focusing on maintenance and upkeep of your properties, offering incentives to tenants, having a good understanding of the local rental market and economy, and building a good relationship with your tenants, you can optimize your rental income and achieve your financial goals.

Another strategy that can help to maximize rental income is to focus on the location of your properties. This includes selecting properties that are in desirable areas, close to public transportation, and near popular amenities such as shopping centers, schools, and parks. By selecting properties in prime locations, you can attract high-quality tenants, increase the appeal of your properties, and increase the rental income potential.

Another important aspect to consider is implementing a rent increase strategy. This can include conducting regular rental evaluations, being transparent with your tenants about any potential rent increases, and increasing rent in a gradual and reasonable manner. By implementing a rent increase strategy, you can increase your rental income while still retaining quality tenants.

Additionally, it's also important to focus on providing a high-quality living experience for your tenants. This can include providing clean and well-maintained properties, offering a variety of amenities, and being responsive to the needs of your tenants. By providing a high-quality living experience, you can attract and retain quality tenants and increase the chances of them renewing their leases.

Finally, it's also important to have a good understanding of the local housing market and economy. This includes being aware of the housing prices, the types of properties that are in demand, and any upcoming developments or trends. By having a good understanding of the local housing market and economy, you can make informed decisions about the rental prices and the type of properties that are in demand.

In conclusion, there are many strategies that can be used to maximize rental income and fill vacancies. By implementing a combination of these techniques and constantly evaluating and adapting your approach, you can create a successful rental property business that provides a steady stream of rental income and the potential for long-term financial freedom. By focusing on the location of your properties, implementing a rent increase strategy, providing a high-quality living experience, and having a good understanding of the local housing market and economy, you can optimize your rental income and achieve your financial goals.

Another strategy to consider is focusing on building a strong brand for your rental properties. This can include creating a consistent message and aesthetic across your properties, using a professional logo and branding materials, and building a strong online presence. By building a strong brand, you can increase the visibility and appeal of your properties, and make it easier to attract and retain quality tenants.

Another important aspect to consider is investing in property upgrades and improvements. This can include modernizing appliances, updating fixtures, and making energy-efficient upgrades. By investing in property upgrades and improvements, you can increase the appeal of your properties, attract high-quality tenants, and increase the rental income potential.

Additionally, it's also important to have a good understanding of the different types of tenants and their needs. This includes understanding the needs of families, students, professionals, retirees, and other types of renters. By having a good understanding of the different types of tenants and their needs, you can make informed decisions about the types of properties to invest in and how to market them.

Finally, it's also important to have a good understanding of the local housing market and economy. This includes being aware of the housing prices, the types of properties that are in demand, and any upcoming developments or trends. By having a good understanding of the local housing market and economy, you can make informed decisions about the rental prices and the type of properties that are in demand.

In conclusion, there are many strategies that can be used to maximize rental income and fill vacancies. By implementing a combination of these techniques and constantly evaluating and adapting your approach, you can create a successful rental property business that provides a steady stream of rental income and the potential for long-term financial freedom. By focusing on building a strong brand, investing in property upgrades and improvements, having a good understanding of the different types of tenants and their needs, and having a good understanding of the local housing market and economy, you can optimize your rental income and achieve your financial goals.


Another strategy to consider is focusing on creating a sense of community among your tenants. This can include hosting events, creating a tenant portal for communication and information sharing, and encouraging tenants to get to know one another. By creating a sense of community among your tenants, you can increase the chances of tenants renewing their leases, and create a positive and desirable living environment for your tenants.

Another important aspect to consider is being proactive in identifying and addressing potential issues with your properties. This can include regular property inspections, being responsive to tenant complaints and concerns, and addressing maintenance and repair issues in a timely manner. By being proactive in identifying and addressing potential issues, you can minimize disruptions and maintain a high-quality living experience for your tenants.

Additionally, it's also important to have a good understanding of the local housing market and economy. This includes being aware of the housing prices, the types of properties that are in demand, and any upcoming developments or trends. By having a good understanding of the local housing market and economy, you can make informed decisions about the rental prices and the type of properties that are in demand.

Finally, it's also important to build a good relationship with your tenants. This can include regularly communicating with them, being responsive to their needs, and being fair and consistent in your dealings with them. By building a good relationship with your tenants, you can increase the chances of them renewing their leases and referring others to your properties.

In conclusion, there are many strategies that can be used to maximize rental income and fill vacancies. By implementing a combination of these techniques and constantly evaluating and adapting your approach, you can create a successful rental property business that provides a steady stream of rental income and the potential for long-term financial freedom. By focusing on creating a sense of community among your tenants, being proactive in identifying and addressing potential issues, having a good understanding of the local housing market and economy, and building a good relationship with your tenants, you can optimize your rental income and achieve your financial goals.

Another strategy to consider is focusing on creating a professional and efficient leasing process. This can include having a clear and detailed application process, conducting background and credit checks, and providing clear and concise lease agreements. By creating a professional and efficient leasing process, you can attract high-quality tenants, reduce the chances of disputes, and increase the chances of tenants renewing their leases.

Another important aspect to consider is having a good understanding of the local housing market and economy. This includes being aware of the housing prices, the types of properties that are in demand, and any upcoming developments or trends. By having a good understanding of the local housing market and economy, you can make informed decisions about the rental prices and the type of properties that are in demand.

Additionally, it's also important to have a good understanding of the different types of tenants and their needs. This includes understanding the needs of families, students, professionals, retirees, and other types of renters. By having a good understanding of the different types of tenants and their needs, you can make informed decisions about the types of properties to invest in and how to market them.

Finally, it's also important to have a good understanding of the local laws and regulations that pertain to rental properties. This includes understanding fair housing laws, eviction procedures, and any other legal requirements that may apply to your rental properties. By staying informed and compliant, you can minimize legal issues and protect your rental income.

In conclusion, there are many strategies that can be used to maximize rental income and fill vacancies. By implementing a combination of these techniques and constantly evaluating and adapting your approach, you can create a successful rental property business that provides a steady stream of rental income and the potential for long-term financial freedom. By focusing on creating a professional and efficient leasing process, having a good understanding of the local housing market and economy, having a good understanding of the different types of tenants and their needs, and having a good understanding of the local laws and regulations that pertain to rental properties, you can optimize your rental income and achieve your financial goals.

Another strategy to consider is diversifying your rental portfolio. This can include investing in different types of properties, such as single-family homes, multi-unit buildings, or vacation rentals. By diversifying your portfolio, you can spread your risk and increase your income potential.

It's also important to have a good understanding of the local housing market and economy. This includes being aware of the housing prices, the types of properties that are in demand, and any upcoming developments or trends. By having a good understanding of the local housing market and economy, you can make informed decisions about the rental prices and the type of properties that are in demand.

Finally, it's also important to have a good understanding of the local laws and regulations that pertain to rental properties. This includes understanding fair housing laws, eviction procedures, and any other legal requirements that may apply to your rental properties. By staying informed and compliant, you can minimize legal issues and protect your rental income.

In conclusion, there are many strategies that can be used to maximize rental income and fill vacancies. By implementing a combination of these techniques and constantly evaluating and adapting your approach, you can create a successful rental property business that provides a steady stream of rental income and the potential for long-term financial freedom. By creating a strong online presence, providing excellent customer service, diversifying your rental portfolio, having a good understanding of the local housing market and economy, and having a good understanding of the local laws and regulations that pertain to rental properties, you can optimize your rental income and achieve your financial goals.

Another strategy to consider is focusing on providing a personalized experience for your tenants. This can include offering custom lease agreements, providing flexible move-in and move-out dates, and offering add-on services such as cleaning or furniture rental. By providing a personalized experience, you can attract and retain high-quality tenants and increase tenant satisfaction.

Another important aspect to consider is implementing a property management system. This can include using software to track and manage properties, tenants, and finances. By implementing a property management system, you can streamline your business operations, increase efficiency and productivity, and make it easier to track and analyze your rental income and expenses.

Additionally, it's also important to stay up to date with the latest technology and trends in the real estate industry. This includes using virtual tours, video rentals, and digital signing to attract and retain tenants, and using data analysis and other tools to make informed decisions about your properties.

Finally, it's also important to have a good understanding of the local housing market and economy. This includes being aware of the housing prices, the types of properties that are in demand, and any upcoming developments or trends. By having a good understanding of the local housing market and economy, you can make informed decisions about the rental prices and the type of properties that are in demand.

In conclusion, there are many strategies that can be used to maximize rental income and fill vacancies. By implementing a combination of these techniques and constantly evaluating and adapting your approach, you can create a successful rental property business that provides a steady stream of rental income and the potential for long-term financial freedom. By focusing on providing a personalized experience, implementing a property management system, staying up to date with the latest technology and trends in the real estate industry, and having a good understanding of the local housing market and economy, you can optimize your rental income and achieve your financial goals.

Another strategy to consider is focusing on building a strong team of professionals to support your rental property business. This can include hiring a property manager, a real estate attorney, an accountant, and other professionals who can help you with the legal, financial, and operational aspects of your business. By building a strong team, you can increase the efficiency and effectiveness of your business and make it easier to manage your properties and tenants.

Another important aspect to consider is investing in technology and tools that can help you manage your rental properties. This can include using property management software, online rental platforms, and mobile apps that can help you manage your properties, communicate with tenants, and collect rent payments. By investing in technology and tools, you can increase the efficiency and productivity of your business and make it easier to manage your properties.

Additionally, it's also important to focus on building a positive reputation and brand for your rental properties. This can include offering high-quality properties, providing excellent customer service, and being transparent and honest in your dealings with tenants. By building a positive reputation and brand, you can increase the appeal of your properties and attract high-quality tenants.

Finally, it's also important to stay informed and up-to-date with the latest trends and regulations in the real estate industry. This includes staying informed of changes in housing laws and regulations, staying informed of local housing market trends, and staying informed of the latest technology and tools available to rental property owners. By staying informed and up-to-date, you can make informed decisions and adapt to changes in the industry.

In conclusion, there are many strategies that can be used to maximize rental income and fill vacancies. By implementing a combination of these techniques and constantly evaluating and adapting your approach, you can create a successful rental property business that provides a steady stream of rental income and the potential for long-term financial freedom. By building a strong team, investing in technology and tools, focusing on building a positive reputation and brand, and staying informed and up-to-date with the latest trends and regulations in the real estate industry, you can optimize your rental income and achieve your financial goals.

Another strategy to consider is focusing on creating a seamless and user-friendly tenant experience. This can include offering online rent payments, providing easy access to maintenance requests, and offering a mobile-friendly tenant portal. By creating a seamless and user-friendly tenant experience, you can attract and retain high-quality tenants and increase tenant satisfaction.

Another important aspect to consider is creating a comprehensive marketing strategy to promote your properties. This can include using social media, online advertising, and traditional marketing techniques to reach potential tenants. By creating a comprehensive marketing strategy, you can increase the visibility and appeal of your properties and make it easier to fill vacancies.

Additionally, it's also important to focus on building a strong network of contacts within the real estate industry. This can include building relationships with real estate agents, property managers, and other industry professionals. By building a strong network of contacts, you can gain access to valuable resources and information, and make it easier to find and acquire new properties.

Finally, it's also important to focus on continuous learning and professional development. This can include attending industry conferences, reading industry publications, and taking courses to stay informed about the latest trends and best practices in the real estate industry. By focusing on continuous learning and professional development, you can increase your knowledge and skills, and improve your ability to manage and grow your rental property business.

In conclusion, there are many strategies that can be used to maximize rental income and fill vacancies. By implementing a combination of these techniques and constantly evaluating and adapting your approach, you can create a successful rental property business that provides a steady stream of rental income and the potential for long-term financial freedom. By creating a seamless and user-friendly tenant experience, creating a comprehensive marketing strategy, building a strong network of contacts, and focusing on continuous learning and professional development, you can optimize your rental income and achieve your financial goals.

Another strategy to consider is focusing on building a strong relationship with your tenants. This can include regularly communicating with them, being responsive to their needs, and being fair and consistent in your dealings with them. By building a strong relationship with your tenants, you can increase their satisfaction and retention, and increase the chances of them renewing their leases and referring others to your properties.

Another important aspect to consider is implementing a preventative maintenance program. This can include regular inspections of your properties, identifying and addressing potential issues before they become major problems, and providing regular upkeep and maintenance of the properties. By implementing a preventative maintenance program, you can increase the longevity and value of your properties and decrease the chances of costly repairs.

Additionally, it's also important to be aware of and comply with all local and state laws and regulations that pertain to rental properties. This includes understanding fair housing laws, eviction procedures, and any other legal requirements that may apply to your rental properties. By staying informed and compliant, you can minimize legal issues and protect your rental income.

Finally, it's also important to focus on continuing your education and staying informed of the latest industry trends and best practices. This can include attending industry conferences, joining professional organizations, and reading industry publications. By staying informed and educated, you can improve your ability to manage and grow your rental property business.

In conclusion, there are many strategies that can be used to maximize rental income and fill vacancies. By implementing a combination of these techniques and constantly evaluating and adapting your approach, you can create a successful rental property business that provides a steady stream of rental income and the potential for long-term financial freedom. By building a strong relationship with your tenants, implementing a preventative maintenance program, being aware of and complying with all local and state laws and regulations, and focusing on continuing your education and staying informed of the latest industry trends and best practices, you can optimize your rental income and achieve your financial goals.


Another strategy to consider is focusing on creating a welcoming and inviting atmosphere in your rental properties. This can include decorating the properties with stylish and modern furnishings, keeping the properties clean and well-maintained, and providing amenities such as laundry facilities, off-street parking, and access to public transportation. By creating a welcoming and inviting atmosphere, you can attract high-quality tenants and increase the chances of filling vacancies quickly.

Another important aspect to consider is offering flexible leasing options. This can include offering short-term leases, month-to-month leases, and flexible lease start dates. By offering flexible leasing options, you can attract a wider range of tenants and increase the chances of filling vacancies.

Additionally, it's also important to be aware of and respond to tenant feedback and concerns. This includes regularly communicating with tenants, addressing any issues or complaints in a timely manner, and being open to suggestions and feedback. By being responsive to tenant feedback and concerns, you can increase tenant satisfaction and retention.

Finally, it's also important to have a plan in place for dealing with delinquent tenants. This can include having a clear and consistent late-payment policy, and having a process in place for dealing with eviction if necessary. By having a plan in place for dealing with delinquent tenants, you can minimize financial losses and protect your rental income.

In conclusion, there are many strategies that can be used to maximize rental income and fill vacancies. By implementing a combination of these techniques and constantly evaluating and adapting your approach, you can create a successful rental property business that provides a steady stream of rental income and the potential for long-term financial freedom. By creating a welcoming and inviting atmosphere, offering flexible leasing options, being aware of and responsive to tenant feedback and concerns, and having a plan in place for dealing with delinquent tenants, you can optimize your rental income and achieve your financial goals.

Another strategy to consider is focusing on creating a sense of community among your tenants. This can include hosting events such as tenant appreciation parties, encouraging tenants to interact with one another, and providing shared spaces such as a community garden or lounge area. By creating a sense of community, you can increase tenant satisfaction and retention, and create a more desirable living environment.

Another important aspect to consider is offering incentives to tenants. This can include offering discounts on rent for long-term leases, offering a referral program for new tenants, and providing rewards for good tenant behavior such as on-time rent payments. By offering incentives, you can attract and retain high-quality tenants and increase the chances of filling vacancies.

Additionally, it's also important to conduct regular market research to stay informed about the local rental market. This includes monitoring the prices and availability of similar properties in the area, and staying informed about local trends and demand. By conducting regular market research, you can make informed decisions about rental prices and increase your chances of filling vacancies.

Finally, it's also important to focus on providing exceptional customer service to your tenants. This includes being responsive to tenant inquiries and concerns, providing clear and timely communication, and being approachable and easy to work with. By providing exceptional customer service, you can increase tenant satisfaction and retention, and increase the chances of tenants referring others to your properties.

In conclusion, there are many strategies that can be used to maximize rental income and fill vacancies. By implementing a combination of these techniques and constantly evaluating and adapting your approach, you can create a successful rental property business that provides a steady stream of rental income and the potential for long-term financial freedom. By creating a sense of community among your tenants, offering incentives, conducting regular market research, and providing exceptional customer service, you can optimize your rental income and achieve your financial goals.

green energy solutions, such as solar panels or energy-efficient appliances, and incorporating environmentally-friendly practices into the maintenance and upkeep of your properties. By creating energy-efficient and sustainable rental properties, you can not only help protect the environment, but also save money on energy costs and attract eco-conscious tenants. Plus, it's a great way to show that you care about the well-being of your tenants and the planet.

In addition, it's also important to be open to negotiation and flexibility when it comes to rental terms. This can include being willing to negotiate rent prices, offering flexible lease terms, and being open to the idea of renting to pets or allowing subletting. By being open to negotiation and flexibility, you can attract a wider range of tenants and increase the chances of filling vacancies.

Another strategy to consider is creating a sense of security in your rental properties. This can include installing security cameras, providing secure entry systems, and ensuring that your properties are well-lit. By creating a sense of security, you can attract tenants who value safety and peace of mind, and increase the chances of filling vacancies.

In conclusion, there are many strategies that can be used to maximize rental income and fill vacancies. By implementing a combination of these techniques and constantly evaluating and adapting your approach, you can create a successful rental property business that provides a steady stream of rental income and the potential for long-term financial freedom. By creating a strong online presence, providing detailed and accurate information about your properties, having a solid screening process, having a clear and concise lease agreement, creating energy-efficient and sustainable rental properties, being open to negotiation and flexibility, and creating a sense of security, you can optimize your rental income and achieve your financial goals.

Another great strategy to consider is offering additional services to tenants. This can include providing cleaning services, laundry services, or even offering a concierge service to help with errands and tasks. By offering additional services, you can attract tenants who value convenience and ease of living, and increase tenant satisfaction and retention.

Another important aspect to consider is building a strong reputation as a landlord. This can include being responsive to tenant needs, addressing issues and complaints in a timely manner, and being a fair and respectful landlord. By building a strong reputation, you can attract high-quality tenants and increase the chances of filling vacancies.

Additionally, it's also important to stay informed about local and national rental laws and regulations. This includes understanding fair housing laws, eviction procedures, and other legal requirements that may apply to your rental properties. By staying informed and compliant, you can minimize legal issues and protect your rental income.

Finally, it's also important to have a solid plan in place for emergencies. This can include having a list of emergency contact numbers, having a plan in place for dealing with natural disasters, and providing information to tenants on how to handle emergencies. By having a solid emergency plan in place, you can protect the safety of your tenants and minimize damage to your properties.

In conclusion, there are many strategies that can be used to maximize rental income and fill vacancies. By implementing a combination of these techniques and constantly evaluating and adapting your approach, you can create a successful rental property business that provides a steady stream of rental income and the potential for long-term financial freedom. By offering additional services, building a strong reputation, staying informed about local and national rental laws and regulations, and having a solid plan in place for emergencies, you can optimize your rental income and achieve your financial goals.

Another strategy to consider is focusing on creating a sense of luxury in your rental properties. This can include upgrading the finishes and fixtures in your properties, providing high-end amenities, and creating a sense of elegance and exclusivity. By creating a sense of luxury, you can attract tenants who value the finer things in life and are willing to pay a premium for them.

Another important aspect to consider is providing value-added services to your tenants. This can include offering a concierge service, providing on-site maintenance, and offering a rewards program for good tenant behavior. By providing value-added services, you can attract tenants who value convenience and ease of living, and increase tenant satisfaction and retention.

Additionally, it's also important to have a solid plan in place for property management. This includes having a system in place for handling tenant complaints, managing maintenance and repairs, and maintaining accurate financial records. By having a solid plan in place for property management, you can minimize the stress and workload of managing rental properties.

In conclusion, there are many strategies that can be used to maximize rental income and fill vacancies. By implementing a combination of these techniques and constantly evaluating and adapting your approach, you can create a successful rental property business that provides a steady stream of rental income and the potential for long-term financial freedom. By creating a sense of luxury, providing value-added services, having a solid plan in place for property management, and creating a sense of community, you can optimize your rental income and achieve your financial goals.

*"The key to creating a successful rental property business is not just about finding the right properties, but also about implementing strategies to maximize rental income and fill vacancies through an approach that is constantly evaluated and adapted"*

## Notes

..................................................................................................

..................................................................................................

..................................................................................................

# Chapter 4: Managing Rental Properties: Tips for Effective Property Management and Maintenance

Managing rental properties can be a daunting task, but with the right approach and strategies, it can be a profitable and rewarding endeavor. In this chapter, we will discuss tips for effective property management and maintenance that can help you navigate the day-to-day responsibilities of being a landlord.

First and foremost, it's important to have a solid plan in place for property management. This includes having a system in place for handling tenant complaints, managing maintenance and repairs, and maintaining accurate financial records. By having a solid plan in place for property management, you can minimize the stress and workload of managing rental properties.

One important aspect of property management is regular maintenance and upkeep of your properties. This includes ensuring that all appliances and systems are in good working order, making necessary repairs, and keeping the properties clean and well-maintained. By providing regular maintenance, you can increase the lifespan of your properties, attract high-quality tenants, and increase tenant satisfaction and retention.

Another important aspect of property management is effectively communicating with your tenants. This includes providing clear and timely communication, being responsive to tenant inquiries and concerns, and being approachable and easy to work with. By providing effective communication, you can increase tenant satisfaction and retention, and minimize misunderstandings and conflicts.

Additionally, it's also important to have a clear and concise lease agreement in place. This includes outlining the responsibilities of the tenant and the landlord, providing information on the rent and security deposit, and outlining the process for handling maintenance and repairs. By having a clear and concise lease agreement in place, you can minimize misunderstandings and conflicts between the landlord and tenant, and protect your legal rights as a landlord.

Another important aspect of property management is understanding and complying with local and national rental laws and regulations. This includes understanding fair housing laws, eviction procedures, and other legal requirements that may apply to your rental properties. By staying informed and compliant, you can minimize legal issues and protect your rental income.

In conclusion, managing rental properties requires a balance of effective property management and maintenance, good communication with tenants, a clear and concise lease agreement, and knowledge of the local and national rental laws and regulations. By following these guidelines, you can ensure that your rental properties are well-maintained, your tenants are happy and satisfied, and you are able to protect your rental income.

"Effective property management is not just about maintaining the property, but also about understanding and complying with the local and national laws and regulations, maintaining a good communication with tenants, and having a clear and concise lease agreement in place"

Another important aspect of property management is handling tenant turnover. This includes preparing properties for new tenants, conducting move-in and move-out inspections, and handling security deposit refunds. By having a system in place for handling tenant turnover, you can minimize vacancies and ensure that your properties are always generating rental income.

Another important aspect of property management is understanding and managing rental finances. This includes collecting rent, managing expenses, and keeping accurate financial records. By understanding and managing rental finances, you can ensure that your rental properties are profitable and that you have a clear understanding of your financial situation.

Another important aspect of property management is understanding and managing the local rental market. This includes staying informed about the prices and availability of similar properties in the area, and staying informed about local trends and demand. By understanding and managing the local rental market, you can make informed decisions about rental prices, increase your chances of filling vacancies, and ensure that your properties are competitive in the market.

Additionally, it's also important to have a plan in place for emergencies. This can include having a list of emergency contact numbers, having a plan in place for dealing with natural disasters, and providing information to tenants on how to handle emergencies. By having a plan in place for emergencies, you can protect the safety of your tenants and minimize damage to your properties.

Another important aspect of property management is providing exceptional customer service to your tenants. This includes being responsive to tenant inquiries and concerns, providing clear and timely communication, and being approachable and easy to work with. By providing exceptional customer service, you can increase tenant satisfaction and retention, and increase the chances of tenants referring others to your properties.

In conclusion, managing rental properties requires a balance of effective property management and maintenance, good communication with tenants, a clear and concise lease agreement, knowledge of the local and national rental laws and regulations, handling tenant turnover, managing rental finances, managing the local rental market, having a plan in place for emergencies, and providing exceptional customer service. By following these guidelines, you can ensure that your rental properties are well-maintained, your tenants are happy and satisfied, and you are able to protect your rental income.

Another strategy to consider when managing rental properties is outsourcing certain tasks to professionals. This can include hiring a property management company to handle day-to-day responsibilities, hiring a cleaning or maintenance company to handle regular upkeep, or hiring an accountant to handle financial management. By outsourcing certain tasks, you can save time and reduce stress, allowing you to focus on other aspects of your business.

Another important aspect of property management is ensuring that your properties are safe and comply with safety regulations. This includes ensuring that all appliances and systems are in good working order, making necessary repairs, and ensuring that your properties comply with local building codes and safety regulations. By providing regular maintenance and ensuring safety, you can attract high-quality tenants, increase tenant satisfaction, and minimize legal issues.

Another strategy to consider is implementing technology in your property management business. This can include using software to manage tenant information, automate rent collection, and track maintenance requests. By implementing technology, you can streamline processes, increase efficiency, and reduce errors.

In addition, it's also important to be aware of potential hazards and risks when managing rental properties. This includes being aware of potential hazards such as lead paint or mold, and having a plan in place to address them. By being aware of potential hazards and having a plan in place, you can minimize risks, protect your tenants, and protect your business.

In conclusion, managing rental properties requires a balance of effective property management and maintenance, good communication with tenants, a clear and concise lease agreement, knowledge of the local and national rental laws and regulations, handling tenant turnover, managing rental finances, managing the local rental market, having a plan in place for emergencies, providing exceptional customer service, outsourcing certain tasks, ensuring safety regulations are met and implementing technology to help streamline processes. By following these guidelines, you can ensure that your rental properties are well-maintained, your tenants are happy and satisfied, and you are able to protect your rental income. One important aspect of property management is understanding the importance of having proper insurance coverage. This includes having insurance to protect your properties from damage or loss, and having liability insurance to protect you from lawsuits or claims. By having proper insurance coverage, you can minimize financial risks and protect your business in case of an accident or disaster.

Another important aspect of property management is understanding the importance of networking and building relationships. This includes building relationships with other landlords, real estate professionals, and service providers. By networking and building relationships, you can gain access to valuable resources, advice and support, and increase your chances of finding new properties, tenants, and opportunities.

Another strategy to consider is being proactive in your approach to property management. This includes being proactive in your marketing and advertising efforts, conducting regular inspections of your properties, and being proactive in addressing any issues or concerns that may arise. By being proactive, you can minimize potential problems, increase tenant satisfaction and retention, and increase the overall success of your business.

In addition, it's also important to be aware of the latest trends and developments in the rental market. This includes staying informed about the latest technologies, marketing strategies, and legal changes that may impact your business. By staying informed and adapting to changes, you can ensure that your business is competitive and successful.

In conclusion, managing rental properties requires a balance of effective property management and maintenance, good communication with tenants, a clear and concise lease agreement, knowledge of the local and national rental laws and regulations, handling tenant turnover, managing rental finances, managing the local rental market, having a plan in place for emergencies, providing exceptional customer service, outsourcing certain tasks, ensuring safety regulations are met, implementing technology, having proper insurance coverage, networking and building relationships, and being proactive and informed about the latest trends and developments in the rental market. By following these guidelines, you can ensure that your rental properties are well-maintained, your tenants are happy and satisfied, and you are able to protect your rental income.

Another key aspect of property management is understanding the importance of being organized and efficient. This includes having a system in place for keeping track of important documents such as leases and contracts, keeping accurate records of income and expenses, and having a schedule for regular maintenance and inspections. By being organized and efficient, you can save time, reduce stress, and ensure that your business runs smoothly.

Another strategy to consider is offering incentives to tenants. This can include offering discounts or rewards for on-time rent payments, renewing leases or referring new tenants. By offering incentives, you can increase tenant satisfaction and retention, and attract new tenants to your properties.

Another important aspect of property management is understanding how to handle difficult tenants. This includes having a plan in place for addressing late rent payments, dealing with noise complaints, and handling evictions. By understanding how to handle difficult tenants, you can minimize legal issues and protect your business.

In addition, it's also important to have a budget in place for managing your rental properties. This includes having a plan for managing expenses, setting aside money for repairs and maintenance, and having a plan for unexpected costs. By having a budget in place, you can ensure that your rental properties are financially stable, and you can make informed decisions about your business.

In conclusion, managing rental properties requires a balance of effective property management and maintenance, good communication with tenants, a clear and concise lease agreement, knowledge of the local and national rental laws and regulations, handling tenant turnover, managing rental finances, managing the local rental market, having a plan in place for emergencies, providing exceptional customer service, outsourcing certain tasks, ensuring safety regulations are met, implementing technology, having proper insurance coverage, networking and building relationships, being proactive and informed about the latest trends and developments in the rental market, being organized and efficient, offering incentives to tenants, understanding how to handle difficult tenants and having a budget in place to manage expenses. By following these guidelines, you can ensure that your rental properties are well-maintained, your tenants are happy and satisfied, and you are able to protect your rental income.

Another important aspect of property management is understanding the importance of marketing and advertising your properties. This includes creating effective listings, using online platforms to reach potential tenants, and using traditional marketing methods such as print ads or open houses. By effectively marketing and advertising your properties, you can increase your chances of filling vacancies and reaching potential tenants.

Another important aspect of property management is understanding the importance of building a strong online presence. This includes having a professional website, active social media accounts, and positive reviews and testimonials from previous tenants. By building a strong online presence, you can increase your visibility, attract new tenants, and establish trust and credibility with potential tenants.

Another strategy to consider is offering additional services to your tenants. This can include offering paid amenities such as parking, storage, or laundry facilities. By offering additional services, you can increase your rental income and attract high-paying tenants to your properties.

In addition, it's also important to be aware of the tax implications of owning rental properties. This includes understanding the deductions and credits available, keeping accurate records of income and expenses, and consulting with a tax professional to ensure compliance with local, state, and federal laws. By being aware of the tax implications, you can minimize your tax liability and protect your rental income.

In conclusion, managing rental properties requires a balance of effective property management and maintenance, good communication with tenants, a clear and concise lease agreement, knowledge of the local and national rental laws and regulations, handling tenant turnover, managing rental finances, managing the local rental market, having a plan in place for emergencies, providing exceptional customer service, outsourcing certain tasks, ensuring safety regulations are met, implementing technology, having proper insurance coverage, networking and building relationships, being proactive and informed about the latest trends and developments in the rental market, being organized and efficient, offering incentives to tenants, understanding how to handle difficult tenants, having a budget in place to manage expenses, effectively marketing and advertising your properties, building a strong online presence, offering additional services to tenants and being aware of the tax implications of owning rental properties. By following these guidelines, you can ensure that your rental properties are well-maintained, your tenants are happy and satisfied, and you are able to protect your rental income.

Another important aspect of property management is understanding the importance of building a strong team. This includes hiring and training employees, delegating tasks and responsibilities, and fostering a positive and supportive work environment. By building a strong team, you can increase efficiency and productivity, and ensure that your business runs smoothly.

Another strategy to consider is diversifying your rental portfolio. This includes investing in different types of rental properties, such as single-family homes, apartments, or commercial properties. By diversifying your portfolio, you can minimize risk and increase your chances of generating consistent rental income.

Another important aspect of property management is understanding the importance of staying up-to-date with local and national laws and regulations. This includes staying informed about tenant rights, fair housing laws, and eviction laws. By staying informed and compliant with laws and regulations, you can minimize legal issues and protect your business.

In addition, it's also important to be aware of the importance of long-term planning. This includes setting long-term goals, developing a strategic plan, and regularly reviewing and adjusting your plan as needed. By having a long-term plan in place, you can ensure that your business is sustainable and successful in the long-term.

In conclusion, managing rental properties requires a balance of effective property management and maintenance, good communication with tenants, a clear and concise lease agreement, knowledge of the local and national rental laws and regulations, handling tenant turnover, managing rental finances, managing the local rental market, having a plan in place for emergencies, providing exceptional customer service, outsourcing certain tasks, ensuring safety regulations are met, implementing technology, having proper insurance coverage, networking and building relationships, being proactive and informed about the latest trends and developments in the rental market, being organized and efficient, offering incentives to tenants, understanding how to handle difficult tenants, having a budget in place to manage expenses, effectively marketing and advertising your properties, building a strong

online presence, offering additional services to tenants, being aware of the tax implications of owning rental properties, building a strong team, diversifying your rental portfolio, staying up-to-date with local and national laws and regulations and having a long-term plan in place. By following these

Another key aspect of property management is understanding the importance of building relationships with local contractors and vendors. This includes finding reliable and affordable service providers for repairs and maintenance, and building relationships with local real estate agents and home inspectors. By building relationships with local contractors and vendors, you can ensure that your properties are well-maintained, and you can save time and money by having access to a network of trusted professionals.

Another strategy to consider is creating a crisis management plan. This includes having a plan in place for dealing with natural disasters, fires, or other emergencies that may affect your properties. By having a crisis management plan in place, you can minimize damage and protect your properties, tenants, and business.

Another important aspect of property management is understanding the importance of building a reputation as a responsible and professional landlord. This includes treating your tenants with respect, responding to their concerns and complaints in a timely manner, and maintaining your properties to a high standard. By building a reputation as a responsible and professional landlord, you can attract high-quality tenants, increase tenant retention, and protect your business.

In addition, it's also important to be aware of the importance of continuing education and professional development. This includes staying informed about the latest trends, technologies, and best practices in the rental industry. By continuing to learn and grow as a property manager, you can stay competitive, improve your skills, and increase the success of your business.

In conclusion, managing rental properties requires a balance of effective property management and maintenance, good communication with tenants, a clear and concise lease agreement, knowledge of the local and national rental laws and regulations, handling tenant turnover, managing rental finances, managing the local rental market, having a plan in place for emergencies, providing exceptional customer service, outsourcing certain tasks, ensuring safety regulations are met, implementing technology, having proper insurance coverage, networking and building relationships, being proactive and informed about the latest trends and developments in the rental market, being organized and efficient, offering incentives to tenants, understanding how to handle difficult tenants, having a budget in place to manage expenses, effectively marketing and advertising your properties, building a strong

online presence, offering additional services to tenants, being aware of the tax implications of owning rental properties, building a strong team, diversifying your rental portfolio, staying up-to-date with local and national laws and regulations, having a long-term plan in place, building relationships with local contractors and vendors, creating a crisis management plan, building a reputation as a responsible and professional landlord and continuing education and professional development. By following these guidelines, you can ensure that your rental properties are well-maintained, your tenants are happy and satisfied, and you are able to protect your rental income.

Another key aspect of property management is understanding the importance of being adaptable and flexible. This includes being open to new ideas, technologies, and strategies, and being willing to make changes as needed. By being adaptable and flexible, you can stay ahead of the competition and continuously improve the performance of your business.

Another strategy to consider is implementing technology to streamline your property management process. This includes using software to manage tenant information, automate rent collection, and track maintenance and repair requests. By implementing technology, you can save time, increase efficiency, and reduce errors.

Another important aspect of property management is understanding the importance of being a good listener and problem-solver. This includes actively listening to your tenants, understanding their concerns and needs, and finding creative solutions to any issues that may arise. By being a good listener and problem-solver, you can increase tenant satisfaction and retention.

In addition, it's also important to be aware of the importance of self-care and work-life balance. This includes taking care of your physical and mental well-being, setting boundaries, and making time for yourself and your family. By taking care of yourself, you can reduce stress, increase productivity, and maintain a healthy and successful business.

In conclusion, managing rental properties requires a balance of effective property management and maintenance, good communication with tenants, a clear and concise lease agreement, knowledge of the local and national rental laws and regulations, handling tenant turnover, managing rental finances, managing the local rental market, having a plan in place for emergencies, providing exceptional customer service, outsourcing certain tasks, ensuring safety regulations are met, implementing technology, having proper insurance coverage, networking and building relationships, being proactive and informed about the latest trends and developments in the rental market, being organized and efficient, offering incentives to tenants, understanding how to handle difficult tenants, having a budget in place to manage expenses, effectively marketing and advertising your properties, building a strong

online presence, offering additional services to tenants, being aware of the tax implications of owning rental properties, building a strong team, diversifying your rental portfolio, staying up-to-date with local and national laws and regulations, having a long-term plan in place, building relationships with local contractors and vendors, creating a crisis management plan, building a reputation as a responsible and professional landlord, continuing education and professional development, being adaptable and flexible, implementing technology to streamline the property management process, being a good listener and problem-solver and taking care of self-care and work-life balance. By following these guidelines, you can ensure that your rental properties are well-maintained, your tenants are happy and satisfied, and you are able to protect your rental income.

Another key aspect of property management is understanding the importance of networking and building relationships within the industry. This includes attending local real estate events, joining industry associations, and connecting with other property managers and landlords. By networking and building relationships, you can gain valuable insights, learn from others' experiences, and stay informed about the latest trends and developments in the industry.

Another strategy to consider is implementing a preventive maintenance plan for your properties. This includes regular inspections, routine repairs and upkeep, and identifying and addressing potential issues before they become major problems. By implementing a preventive maintenance plan, you can reduce costs, increase the longevity of your properties, and provide a safe and comfortable living environment for your tenants.

Another important aspect of property management is understanding the importance of clear and open communication. This includes providing timely and accurate information to your tenants, addressing their concerns in a timely manner, and providing regular updates on any issues or changes that may affect them. By maintaining clear and open communication, you can build trust and credibility with your tenants and increase tenant satisfaction.

In addition, it's also important to be aware of the importance of a good work ethic and professional demeanor. This includes being reliable, dependable, and responsive, and maintaining a positive attitude. By maintaining a good work ethic and professional demeanor, you can establish trust and credibility with your tenants and build a reputation as a responsible and professional landlord.

In conclusion, managing rental properties requires a balance of effective property management and maintenance, good communication with tenants, a clear and concise lease agreement, knowledge of the local and national rental laws and regulations, handling tenant turnover, managing rental finances, managing the local rental market, having a plan in place for emergencies, providing exceptional customer service, outsourcing certain tasks, ensuring safety regulations are met, implementing technology, having proper insurance coverage, networking and building relationships, being proactive and informed about the latest trends and developments in the rental market, being organized and efficient, offering incentives to tenants, understanding how to handle difficult tenants, having a budget in place to manage expenses, effectively marketing and advertising your properties, building a strong online presence, offering additional services to tenants, being aware of the tax implications of owning rental properties, building a strong team, diversifying your rental portfolio, staying up-to-date with local and national laws and regulations, having a long-term plan in place, building relationships with local contractors and vendors, creating a crisis management plan, building a reputation as a responsible and professional landlord, continuing education and professional development, being adaptable and flexible, implementing technology to streamline the property management process, being a good listener and problem-solver, taking care of self-care and work-life balance, networking and building relationships within the industry, implementing a preventive maintenance plan, maintaining clear and open communication and having a good work ethic and professional demeanor. By following these guidelines, you can ensure that your rental properties are well-maintained, your tenants are happy and satisfied, and you are able to protect your rental income.

Another key aspect of property management is understanding the importance of tenant screening and selection. This includes thoroughly vetting potential tenants, checking references and credit scores, and ensuring that they meet the requirements outlined in your lease agreement. By implementing a thorough tenant screening process, you can increase the chances of selecting responsible and reliable tenants, and decrease the likelihood of dealing with tenant issues in the future.

Another strategy to consider is implementing a marketing and advertising plan to promote your properties. This includes creating effective and compelling listings, using various platforms and channels to reach potential tenants, and offering incentives to attract high-quality tenants. By implementing a strong marketing and advertising plan, you can increase occupancy rates and generate consistent rental income.

Another important aspect of property management is understanding the importance of financial management. This includes keeping accurate records, creating a budget, and monitoring expenses to ensure that your business remains profitable. By effectively managing your finances, you can ensure that your business is sustainable in the long-term.

In addition, it's also important to be aware of the importance of providing exceptional customer service. This includes being responsive to tenant needs, addressing concerns and issues in a timely manner, and going above and beyond to ensure their satisfaction. By providing exceptional customer service, you can increase tenant retention and satisfaction, and build a positive reputation for your business.

Another key aspect of property management is understanding the importance of compliance with local and national laws and regulations. This includes staying up-to-date with fair housing laws, safety regulations, and any other laws that pertain to rental properties in your area. By staying compliant with the laws and regulations, you can protect yourself and your business from legal issues and penalties.

Another strategy to consider is implementing a tenant retention plan. This includes offering incentives for long-term tenants, regularly communicating with tenants, and addressing any issues or concerns in a timely manner. By implementing a tenant retention plan, you can reduce turnover and increase rental income.

Another important aspect of property management is understanding the importance of building a strong team. This includes hiring reliable and experienced staff, providing ongoing training, and building a positive and supportive work environment. By building a strong team, you can ensure that your properties are well-maintained, your tenants are satisfied, and your business runs smoothly.

In addition, it's also important to be aware of the importance of building a strong online presence. This includes creating a professional website, maintaining active social media accounts, and promoting your properties through online platforms. By building a strong online presence, you can increase visibility and attract potential tenants.

In conclusion, managing rental properties requires a balance of effective property management and maintenance, good communication with tenants, a clear and concise lease agreement, knowledge of the local and national rental laws and regulations, handling tenant turnover, managing rental finances, managing the local rental market, having a plan in place for emergencies, providing exceptional customer service, outsourcing certain tasks, ensuring safety regulations are met, implementing technology, having proper insurance coverage, networking and building relationships, being proactive and informed about the latest trends and developments in the rental market, being organized and efficient, offering incentives to tenants, understanding how to handle difficult tenants, having a budget in place to manage expenses, effectively marketing and advertising your properties, building a strong online presence, offering additional services to tenants, being aware of the tax implications of owning rental properties, building a strong team, diversifying your rental portfolio, staying up-to-date with local and national laws and regulations, having a long-term plan in place, building relationships with local contractors and vendors, creating a crisis management plan, building a reputation as a responsible and professional landlord, continuing education and professional development, being adaptable and flexible, implementing technology to streamline the property management process, being a good listener and problem-solver, taking care of self-care and work-life balance, networking and building relationships within the industry, implementing a preventive maintenance plan, maintaining clear and open communication, having a good work ethic and professional demeanor, implementing a tenant screening process, implementing a marketing and advertising plan, effectively managing finances, providing exceptional customer service, complying with local and national laws and regulations, implementing a tenant retention plan, building a strong team, and building a strong online presence. By following these guidelines, you can ensure that your rental properties are well-maintained, your tenants are happy and satisfied, and you are able to protect your rental income.

Another key aspect of property management is understanding the importance of risk management. This includes having proper insurance coverage for your properties, creating a crisis management plan, and being prepared for emergencies. By managing risks effectively, you can protect your properties and rental income in the event of unexpected events.

Another strategy to consider is outsourcing certain tasks to professionals. This includes hiring a property management company, an accountant, or a lawyer to handle specific tasks that you may not have the expertise or time to handle yourself. By outsourcing certain tasks, you can focus on the more important aspects of property management and ensure that your properties are well-maintained and your tenants are satisfied.

Another important aspect of property management is understanding the importance of continuing education and professional development. This includes staying up-to-date with the latest trends and developments in the rental market, attending workshops and seminars, and reading relevant books and articles. By staying informed and educated, you can stay competitive in the market and improve your skills as a property manager.

In addition, it's also important to be aware of the importance of being adaptable and flexible. This includes being open to change, being willing to try new things, and being able to adapt to new situations and challenges. By being adaptable and flexible, you can stay competitive in the market and find new opportunities for growth.

Another key aspect of property management is understanding the importance of good record keeping. This includes keeping accurate financial records, maintaining detailed records of repairs and maintenance, and keeping records of all communications with tenants. By keeping accurate records, you can ensure that your properties are well-maintained, your tenants are satisfied, and your business runs smoothly.

Another strategy to consider is offering additional services to tenants. This includes providing amenities such as a gym, a pool, or laundry facilities, or offering additional services such as cleaning or landscaping. By offering additional services, you can attract higher-paying tenants and increase your rental income.

Another important aspect of property management is understanding the importance of networking and building relationships. This includes networking with other property managers, landlords, and professionals in the real estate industry, and building relationships with local contractors and vendors. By networking and building relationships, you can stay informed about the latest trends and developments in the rental market, find new opportunities for growth, and improve your skills as a property manager.

In addition, it's also important to be aware of the importance of taking care of self-care and work-life balance. This includes taking time for yourself, setting boundaries, and making sure that you are not burning out. By taking care of yourself, you can ensure that you are able to handle the demands of property management and maintain a healthy work-life balance.

Another key aspect of property management is understanding the importance of creating a budget and sticking to it. This includes having a plan in place for managing expenses, understanding the costs associated with owning and managing rental properties, and being aware of the tax implications of owning rental properties. By creating a budget and sticking to it, you can ensure that your properties are well-maintained and your business is profitable.

Another strategy to consider is diversifying your rental portfolio. This includes owning different types of properties such as single-family homes, multi-family homes, and commercial properties. By diversifying your rental portfolio, you can reduce risk and increase your chances of success.

Another important aspect of property management is understanding the importance of being a responsible and professional landlord. This includes maintaining a positive reputation within the community, being responsive to tenants' needs, and being a good listener and problem-solver. By being a responsible and professional landlord, you can attract and retain good tenants, and build long-term relationships with your tenants.

In addition, it's also important to be aware of the importance of implementing technology to streamline the property management process. This includes using property management software, digital marketing and advertising tools, and other technologies that can help you manage your properties more efficiently. By implementing technology, you can automate repetitive tasks, increase productivity, and improve communication with tenants.

Another key aspect of property management is understanding the importance of building a strong team. This includes hiring and training a skilled and dedicated staff, building a team of trusted contractors and vendors, and building a team of experts in various fields such as legal, accounting and insurance. By building a strong team, you can ensure that your properties are well-maintained, your tenants are satisfied, and your business runs smoothly.

Another strategy to consider is implementing a tenant retention plan. This includes providing excellent customer service, offering incentives to tenants, and creating a sense of community among tenants. By implementing a tenant retention plan, you can reduce tenant turnover, increase occupancy rates, and increase your rental income.

Another important aspect of property management is understanding the importance of compliance with local and national laws and regulations. This includes understanding and following fair housing laws, building codes, and health and safety regulations. By understanding and following laws and regulations, you can ensure that your properties are safe and comply with legal requirements.

In addition, it's also important to be aware of the importance of marketing and advertising your properties. This includes creating a strong online presence, using digital marketing tools, and building relationships with local real estate agents. By marketing and advertising your properties effectively, you can attract and retain good tenants, and increase your rental income.

Another key aspect of property management is understanding the importance of building a strong online presence. This includes creating a professional website, using social media platforms, and listing your properties on online rental platforms. By building a strong online presence, you can attract potential tenants, increase visibility, and grow your business.

Another strategy to consider is outsourcing certain tasks. This includes hiring a property management company, hiring a bookkeeper, and hiring a marketing agency. By outsourcing certain tasks, you can save time and focus on the most important aspects of property management.

Another important aspect of property management is understanding the importance of continuing education and professional development. This includes attending seminars, workshops, and webinars, reading industry publications, and networking with other property managers. By continuing education and professional development, you can stay up-to-date with the latest trends and developments in the rental market and improve your skills as a property manager.

In addition, it's also important to be aware of the importance of being adaptable and flexible. This includes being open to new ideas, being willing to try new things, and being able to adapt to changing market conditions. By being adaptable and flexible, you can ensure that your properties are well-maintained, your tenants are satisfied, and your business runs smoothly.

In conclusion, managing rental properties requires a balance of effective property management and maintenance, good communication with tenants, a clear and concise lease agreement, knowledge of the local and national rental laws and regulations, handling tenant turnover, managing rental finances, managing the local rental market, having a plan in place for emergencies, providing exceptional customer service, outsourcing certain tasks, ensuring safety regulations are met, implementing technology, having proper insurance coverage, networking and building relationships, being proactive and informed about the latest trends and developments in the rental market, being organized and efficient, offering incentives to tenants, understanding how to handle difficult tenants, having a budget in place to manage expenses, effectively marketing and advertising your properties, building a strong online presence, offering additional services to tenants, being aware of the tax implications of owning rental properties, building a strong team, diversifying your rental portfolio, staying up-to-date with local and national laws and regulations, having a long-term plan in place, building relationships with local contractors and vendors, creating a crisis management plan, building a reputation as a responsible and professional landlord, continuing education and professional development, being adaptable and flexible, implementing technology to streamline the property management process, being a good listener and problem-solver, taking care of self-care and work-life balance, networking and building relationships within the industry, implementing a preventive maintenance plan, maintaining clear and open communication, having a good work ethic and professional demeanor, implementing a tenant screening process, implementing a marketing and advertising plan, effectively managing finances, providing exceptional customer service, complying with local and national laws and regulations, implementing a tenant retention plan, building a strong team, building a strong online presence, managing risks effectively, outsourcing certain tasks, continuing education and professional development, keeping accurate records, offering additional services to tenants, networking and building relationships, taking care of self-care and work-life balance, creating a budget and sticking to it, diversifying your rental portfolio, being a responsible and professional landlord, implementing technology to stream

line the property management process, and building a strong online presence.

Another key aspect of property management is understanding the importance of insurance. This includes having proper insurance coverage for your properties, tenants and business. This will protect you and your assets in case of any unexpected events, such as natural disasters or accidents.

Another strategy to consider is implementing a preventive maintenance plan. This includes regular inspections, routine repairs and upgrades, and staying on top of any potential issues. By implementing a preventive maintenance plan, you can keep your properties in good condition, reduce long-term costs, and increase the value of your properties.

Another important aspect of property management is understanding the importance of keeping accurate records. This includes keeping track of expenses, income, and other important financial information. By keeping accurate records, you can stay on top of your finances, ensure compliance with tax laws, and make informed business decisions.

In addition, it's also important to be aware of the importance of offering additional services to tenants. This includes offering amenities such as on-site laundry, fitness centers, and community spaces. By offering additional services to tenants, you can attract and retain good tenants, increase rental income, and create a sense of community among tenants.

Another key aspect of property management is understanding the importance of networking and building relationships within the industry. This includes attending industry events, joining professional organizations, and networking with other landlords, property managers, and real estate professionals. By networking and building relationships, you can stay informed about the latest trends and developments in the rental market, gain valuable insights, and build a reputation as a responsible and professional landlord.

Another strategy to consider is creating a budget and sticking to it. This includes setting financial goals, creating a budget, and monitoring expenses. By creating a budget and sticking to it, you can manage your finances effectively and ensure that your rental properties are profitable.

Another important aspect of property management is understanding the importance of taking care of self-care and work-life balance. This includes making time for yourself, taking care of your physical and mental health, and setting boundaries between work and personal life. By taking care of self-care and work-life balance, you can reduce stress and burnout and ensure that you are able to manage your rental properties effectively.

In addition, it's also important to be aware of the importance of being organized and efficient. This includes keeping detailed records, setting goals, and creating a schedule. By being organized and efficient, you can save time, increase productivity, and ensure that your rental properties are well-managed.

In conclusion, managing rental properties requires a balance of effective property management and maintenance, good communication with tenants, a clear and concise lease agreement, knowledge of the local and national rental laws and regulations, handling tenant turnover, managing rental finances, managing the local rental market, having a plan in place for emergencies, providing exceptional customer service, outsourcing certain tasks, ensuring safety regulations are met, implementing technology, having proper insurance coverage, networking and building relationships, being proactive and informed about the latest trends and developments in the rental market, being organized and efficient, offering incentives to tenants, understanding how to handle difficult tenants, having a budget in place to manage expenses, effectively marketing and advertising your properties, building a strong online presence, offering additional services to tenants, being aware of the tax implications of owning rental properties, building a strong team, diversifying your rental portfolio, staying up-to-date with local and national laws and regulations, having a long-term plan in place, building relationships with local contractors and vendors, creating a crisis management plan, building a reputation as a responsible and professional landlord, continuing education and professional development, being adaptable and flexible, implementing technology to streamline the property management process, being a good listener and problem-solver, taking care of self-care and work-life balance, networking and building relationships within the industry, implementing a preventive maintenance plan, maintaining clear and open communication, having a good work ethic and professional demeanor, implementing a tenant screening process, implementing a marketing and advertising plan, effectively managing finances, providing exceptional customer service, complying with local and national laws and regulations, implementing a tenant retention plan, building a strong team, building a strong online presence, managing risks effectively, outsourcing certain tasks, continuing education and professional development, keeping accurate records, offering additional services to tenants, networking and building relationships, taking care of self-care and work-life balance, creating a budget and sticking to it, diversifying your rental portfolio, being a responsible and professional landlord, implementing technology to streamline the property management process, building a strong online presence, having proper insurance coverage, implementing a preventive maintenance plan, networking and building relationships within the industry, and taking care of self-care and work-life balance.

Another key aspect of property management is understanding the importance of tenant retention. This includes understanding the reasons why tenants leave, creating a tenant retention plan, and implementing strategies to keep good tenants. By understanding and implementing effective tenant retention strategies, you can reduce tenant turnover, increase rental income, and save on marketing and advertising costs.

Another strategy to consider is diversifying your rental portfolio. This includes investing in different types of rental properties, such as single-family homes, multi-unit buildings, and commercial properties. By diversifying your rental portfolio, you can reduce risk, increase cash flow, and improve the overall performance of your rental properties.

Another important aspect of property management is understanding the importance of marketing and advertising. This includes identifying your target market, developing a marketing plan, and implementing effective advertising strategies. By understanding and implementing effective marketing and advertising strategies, you can attract and retain good tenants, increase visibility, and grow your business.

In conclusion, managing rental properties requires a balance of effective property management and maintenance, good communication with tenants, a clear and concise lease agreement, knowledge of the local and national rental laws and regulations, handling tenant turnover, managing rental finances, managing the local rental market, having a plan in place for emergencies, providing exceptional customer service, outsourcing certain tasks, ensuring safety regulations are met, implementing technology, having proper insurance coverage, networking and building relationships, being proactive and informed about the latest trends and developments in the rental market, being organized and efficient, offering incentives to tenants, understanding how to handle difficult tenants, having a budget in place to manage expenses, effectively marketing and advertising your properties, building a strong online presence, offering additional services to tenants, being aware of the tax implications of owning rental properties, building a strong team, diversifying your rental portfolio, staying up-to-date with local and national laws and regulations, having a long-term plan in place, building relationships with local contractors and vendors, creating a crisis management plan, building a reputation as a responsible and professional landlord, continuing education and professional development, being adaptable and flexible, implementing technology to streamline the property management process, being a good listener and problem-solver, taking care of self-care and work-life balance, networking and building relationships within the industry, implementing a preventive maintenance plan, maintaining clear and open communication, having a good work ethic and professional demeanor, implementing a tenant screening process, implementing a marketing and advertising plan, effectively managing finances, providing exceptional customer service, complying with local and national laws and regulations, implementing a tenant retention plan, building a strong team, building a strong online presence, managing risks effectively, outsourcing certain tasks, continuing education and professional development, keeping accurate records, offering additional services to tenants, networking and building relationships, taking care of self-care and work-life balance, creating a budget and sticking to it, diversifying your rental portfolio, being a responsible and professional landlord.

Managing rental properties is not just about collecting rent and fixing leaks, it's about understanding the potential of real estate rentals for financial freedom, and having a balance of effective property management, good communication with tenants, knowledge of the local and national rental laws, handling tenant turnover, managing rental finances, managing the local rental market, having a plan in place for emergencies, providing exceptional customer service, implementing technology, having proper insurance coverage, networking and building relationships, being organized and efficient, offering incentives to tenants, understanding how to handle difficult tenants, effectively marketing and advertising your properties, building a strong online presence, offering additional services to tenants, being aware of the tax implications of owning rental properties, building a strong team, diversifying your rental portfolio, staying up-to-date with local and national laws, having a long-term plan in place, building relationships with local contractors and vendors, creating a crisis management plan, building a reputation as a responsible and professional landlord, continuing education and professional development, being adaptable and flexible, being a good listener and problem-solver, taking care of self-care and work-life balance, implementing a preventive maintenance plan, and having a budget in place to manage expenses.

*"Managing rental properties is a balance of effective management, communication, and strategy to achieve financial freedom."*

## Notes

- ..............................................................................................
- ..............................................................................................
- ..............................................................................................

# Chapter 5: Building a Rental Portfolio: Strategies for Expanding Your Rental Business and Increasing Income

One of the keys to building a successful rental business is expanding your rental portfolio. This means acquiring additional properties to rent out, and diversifying your portfolio to reduce risk and increase income. In this chapter, we will discuss strategies for building a rental portfolio, and how to increase your income through smart investments.

One strategy for building a rental portfolio is to invest in different types of properties. This includes single-family homes, multi-unit buildings, and commercial properties. By diversifying your portfolio, you can reduce risk and increase cash flow. For example, if you have a portfolio of single-family homes, and one of them becomes vacant, it can have a significant impact on your income. However, if you have a diversified portfolio that includes multiple properties, the impact of a vacancy will be less significant.

Another strategy for building a rental portfolio is to invest in properties in different locations. This can include different cities, states, or even countries. By investing in properties in different locations, you can take advantage of different rental markets and increase your income. For example, if you invest in properties in a city with a strong economy, you can charge higher rent prices and increase your income.

Another strategy for building a rental portfolio is to invest in properties that offer long-term potential. This can include properties that are in areas with potential for growth, such as properties located near new developments or infrastructure projects. By investing in properties that offer long-term potential, you can increase your income over time as the value of the property increases.

Another strategy for building a rental portfolio is to invest in properties that offer additional income potential. This can include properties that can be used for short-term rentals, such as vacation rentals or Airbnb rentals. By investing in properties that offer additional income potential, you can increase your income by renting out the property on a short-term basis.

Another strategy for building a rental portfolio is to invest in properties that are in need of repair or renovation. This can include properties that are in need of repairs or renovations, and that can be purchased at a discounted price. By investing in properties that are in need of repair or renovation, you can increase your income by increasing the value of the property after the repairs or renovations are completed.

In conclusion, building a rental portfolio is an important step in expanding your rental business and increasing income. By investing in different types of properties, investing in properties in different locations, investing in properties that offer long-term potential, investing in properties that offer additional income potential, and investing in properties that are in need of repair or renovation, you can reduce risk and increase your income.

"A diverse rental portfolio is the key to achieving financial stability and security in the long-term."

Another strategy for building a rental portfolio is to invest in properties that have a high demand for rental. This includes properties that are located in areas with good schools, universities, hospitals, and other amenities. By investing in properties that have a high demand for rental, you can ensure that your properties will be occupied and generating income.

Another way to expand your rental business and increase your income is through partnerships and joint ventures. Partnering with other landlords or real estate investors can help you acquire properties that you may not have been able to purchase on your own, and also sharing the workload and expenses. Another way to expand your rental business is to invest in real estate funds or REITs, which allow you to invest in a diversified portfolio of properties without the need to own or manage them.

In addition to acquiring properties, one of the most important strategies for building a rental portfolio is to keep your properties in good condition, so that they are attractive to renters and can command higher rents. This includes performing regular maintenance and repairs, updating appliances, and making any necessary renovations. By keeping your properties in good condition, you can ensure that your properties will be occupied and generating income.

Finally, it is important to keep accurate records of your rental properties, including all the income and expenses for each property, and keeping a copy of all the lease agreements. This will help you keep track of your properties and make informed decisions about your rental business.

In conclusion, building a rental portfolio is an important step in expanding your rental business and increasing income. By investing in different types of properties, investing in properties in different locations, investing in properties that offer long-term potential, investing in properties that offer additional income potential, investing in properties that are in need of repair or renovation, investing in properties that have a high demand for rental, partnering and joint ventures, and investing in real estate funds or REITs, keeping your properties in good condition and keeping accurate records, you can reduce risk and increase your income.

"Building a rental portfolio is like building a puzzle, it requires patience, skill, and the right strategy to create a complete and profitable picture."

Another strategy for building a rental portfolio is to invest in rental properties that offer tax benefits. This includes properties that are located in areas that are eligible for tax incentives such as the Low-Income Housing Tax Credit (LIHTC) program, which provides tax credits to landlords who make their properties available to low-income renters. Additionally, investing in properties that are located in areas that are eligible for depreciation deductions can also be a good way to reduce tax liability.

Another strategy for building a rental portfolio is to invest in properties that offer cash flow. This includes properties that are located in areas with high rental demand and low property taxes. By investing in properties that offer cash flow, you can ensure that your properties will be generating income and that you will have a steady stream of cash flow.

It's also important to be aware of the local market conditions and stay informed about the rental laws, regulations, and trends. This will help you make informed decisions when buying properties, setting rents, and managing your properties.

In addition, building a strong team of professionals such as real estate agents, property managers, attorneys, and accountants can help you navigate the complexities of building a rental portfolio, and also help you take advantage of the opportunities that come your way.

Finally, it's important to have a long-term vision and a plan in place for your rental portfolio. This includes setting clear goals, creating a budget, and regularly reviewing your portfolio to ensure that it is aligned with your goals. By having a long-term vision and a plan in place, you can ensure that your rental portfolio is generating consistent income and providing you with financial freedom.

In conclusion, building a rental portfolio is a process that requires patience, skill, and the right strategy. By investing in different types of properties, investing in properties in different locations, investing in properties that offer long-term potential, investing in properties that offer additional income potential, investing in properties that are in need of repair or renovation, investing in properties that have a high demand for rental, partnering and joint ventures, investing in real estate funds or REITs, keeping your properties in good condition and keeping accurate records, investing in properties that offer tax benefits, investing in properties that offer cash flow, staying informed about the local market conditions, building a strong team of professionals, and having a long-term vision and a plan in place, you can reduce risk and increase your income and achieve financial freedom.

"Building a rental portfolio is like planting a seed, it takes time and care, but when nurtured correctly, it will grow into a thriving income-generating tree"

Another important strategy when building a rental portfolio is to have a good understanding of the financing options available to you. This includes understanding the different types of loans available, such as conventional loans, FHA loans, VA loans, and hard money loans, and how they can be used to acquire properties. It also includes understanding the terms and conditions of the loans, such as the interest rate, fees, and repayment terms. By having a good understanding of the financing options available, you can make informed decisions about how to acquire properties and manage your cash flow.

Another strategy for building a rental portfolio is to invest in properties that offer appreciation potential. This includes properties that are located in areas with strong job growth, population growth, and economic development. By investing in properties that offer appreciation potential, you can increase your income over time as the value of the property increases.

It's also important to be aware of the local rental market conditions, and to stay informed about the rental laws, regulations, and trends. This will help you set the right rent prices, and also make informed decisions about when to buy and sell properties. Keeping track of the local rental market can help you identify the best opportunities for buying and selling rental properties.

Finally, it's important to have a good understanding of the tax implications of owning rental properties, and to work with a qualified tax professional to minimize your tax liability. This includes understanding the tax deductions and credits available to landlords, and taking advantage of them to reduce your tax liability.

In conclusion, building a rental portfolio is a process that requires patience, skill, and the right strategy. By investing in different types of properties, investing in properties in different locations, investing in properties that offer long-term potential, investing in properties that offer additional income potential, investing in properties that are in need of repair or renovation, investing in properties that have a high demand for rental, partnering and joint ventures, investing in real estate funds or REITs, keeping your properties in good condition, keeping accurate records, investing in properties that offer tax benefits, investing in properties that offer cash flow, staying informed about the local market conditions, building a strong team of professionals, having a long-term vision and a plan in place, having a good understanding of the financing options, investing in properties that offer appreciation potential, being aware of the local rental market conditions, and having a good understanding of the tax implications of owning rental properties, you can reduce risk and increase your income and achieve financial freedom.

"Building a rental portfolio is like climbing a mountain, it's challenging but the view from the top is worth the effort"

Another strategy for building a rental portfolio is to invest in properties that offer diversification benefits. This includes investing in properties in different locations, different types of properties such as single-family homes, multi-family homes, and commercial properties, and properties that are in different stages of the rental market cycle. By diversifying your portfolio, you can reduce risk and increase your income by spreading your investments across different areas, types of properties, and stages of the rental market cycle.

Another strategy for building a rental portfolio is to invest in properties that offer cash flow positive from the start. This includes investing in properties that are already generating positive cash flow or have the potential to generate positive cash flow. By investing in properties that offer cash flow positive, you can ensure that your properties will be generating income and that you will have a steady stream of cash flow.

It's also important to have a good understanding of the local rental market conditions, and to stay informed about the rental laws, regulations, and trends. This will help you make informed decisions about when to buy and sell properties, and also make informed decisions about setting rents. Keeping track of the local rental market can help you identify the best opportunities for buying and selling rental properties.

Finally, it's important to have a good understanding of the tax implications of owning rental properties, and to work with a qualified tax professional to minimize your tax liability. This includes understanding the tax deductions and credits available to landlords, and taking advantage of them to reduce your tax liability.

In conclusion, building a rental portfolio is a process that requires patience, skill, and the right strategy. By investing in different types of properties, investing in properties in different locations, investing in properties that offer long-term potential, investing in properties that offer additional income potential, investing in properties that are in need of repair or renovation, investing in properties that have a high demand for rental, partnering and joint ventures, investing in real estate funds or REITs, keeping your properties in good condition and keeping accurate records, investing in properties that offer tax benefits, investing in properties that offer cash flow, staying informed about the local market conditions, building a strong team of professionals, having a long-term vision and a plan in place, having a good understanding of the financing options, investing in properties that offer appreciation potential, being aware of the local rental market conditions, and having a good understanding of the tax implications of owning rental properties, diversifying your portfolio, investing in properties that offer cash flow positive, you can reduce risk and increase your income and achieve financial freedom.

"Building a rental portfolio is like playing a chess game, it requires strategy, foresight, and adaptability to win"

Another strategy for building a rental portfolio is to invest in properties that have the potential for value-add. This includes properties that are in need of repair or renovation, or properties that are under-rented. By investing in properties that have the potential for value-add, you can increase the value of the property and the rental income. This can be done by making necessary repairs or renovations, or by increasing the rent to market value.

Another strategy for building a rental portfolio is to invest in properties that offer long-term potential. This includes properties that are located in areas with strong job growth, population growth, and economic development. By investing in properties that offer long-term potential, you can increase your income over time as the value of the property increases.

It's also important to have a good understanding of the local rental market conditions, and to stay informed about the rental laws, regulations, and trends. This will help you make informed decisions about when to buy and sell properties, and also make informed decisions about setting rents. Keeping track of the local rental market can help you identify the best opportunities for buying and selling rental properties.

Finally, it's important to have a good understanding of the tax implications of owning rental properties, and to work with a qualified tax professional to minimize your tax liability. This includes understanding the tax deductions and credits available to landlords, and taking advantage of them to reduce your tax liability.

In conclusion, building a rental portfolio is a process that requires patience, skill, and the right strategy. By investing in different types of properties, investing in properties in different locations, investing in properties that offer long-term potential, investing in properties that offer additional income potential, investing in properties that are in need of repair or renovation, investing in properties that have a high demand for rental, partnering and joint ventures, investing in real estate funds or REITs, keeping your properties in good condition and keeping accurate records, investing in properties that offer tax benefits, investing in properties that offer cash flow, staying informed about the local market conditions, building a strong team of professionals, having a long-term vision and a plan in place, having a good understanding of the financing options, investing in properties that offer appreciation potential, being aware of the local rental market conditions, and having a good understanding of the tax implications of owning rental properties, diversifying your portfolio, investing in properties that offer cash flow positive, investing in properties that have the potential for value-add, you can reduce risk and increase your income and achieve financial freedom.

"Building a rental portfolio is like building a puzzle, it takes time, effort and patience to put the pieces together, but the finished product is a beautiful picture of financial freedom"

Another strategy for building a rental portfolio is to invest in properties that offer a steady stream of income. This includes properties that are in high demand for rental, such as properties located near universities, hospitals, or transportation hubs. By investing in properties that offer a steady stream of income, you can ensure that your properties will be generating income and that you will have a steady stream of cash flow.

Another strategy for building a rental portfolio is to invest in properties through joint ventures or partnerships. This allows you to pool resources and expertise with other investors, which can help you acquire properties that you may not be able to afford on your own. Additionally, it allows you to share the risk and responsibilities of property management, which can help you reduce the workload and increase your income.

It's also important to have a good understanding of the local rental market conditions, and to stay informed about the rental laws, regulations, and trends. This will help you make informed decisions about when to buy and sell properties, and also make informed decisions about setting rents. Keeping track of the local rental market can help you identify the best opportunities for buying and selling rental properties.

Finally, it's important to have a good understanding of the tax implications of owning rental properties, and to work with a qualified tax professional to minimize your tax liability. This includes understanding the tax deductions and credits available to landlords, and taking advantage of them to reduce your tax liability.

In conclusion, building a rental portfolio is a process that requires patience, skill, and the right strategy. By investing in different types of properties, investing in properties in different locations, investing in properties that offer long-term potential, investing in properties that offer additional income potential, investing in properties that are in need of repair or renovation, investing in properties that have a high demand for rental, partnering and joint ventures, investing in real estate funds or REITs, keeping your properties in good condition and keeping accurate records, investing in properties that offer tax benefits, investing in properties that offer cash flow, staying informed about the local market conditions, building a strong team of professionals, having a long-term vision and a plan in place, having a good understanding of the financing options, investing in properties that offer appreciation potential, being aware of the local rental market conditions, and having a good understanding of the tax implications of owning rental properties, diversifying your portfolio, investing in properties that offer cash flow positive, investing in properties that have the potential for value-add, investing in properties that offer a steady stream of income, you can reduce risk and increase your income and achieve financial freedom.

"Building a rental portfolio is like planting a seed, it takes time, effort and patience to grow, but the end result is a beautiful tree of financial freedom"

And don't forget, it's important to keep your properties in good condition and keep accurate records. This can help you attract and retain tenants, as well as ensure that your properties are running smoothly. It's also important to build a strong team of professionals, such as property managers, accountants, and attorneys, who can help you navigate the complexities of owning rental properties.

Finally, it's important to have a long-term vision and a plan in place. It's important to set goals and objectives and to review your portfolio regularly to ensure that you're on track to achieve your goals. It's also important to be aware of the financing options available to you, so that you can access the capital you need building a rental portfolio is a process that requires patience, skill, and the right strategy. By investing in different types of properties, investing in properties in different locations, investing in properties that offer long-term potential, investing in properties that offer additional income potential, investing in properties that are in need of repair or renovation, investing in properties that have a high demand for rental, partnering and joint ventures, investing in real estate funds or REITs, keeping your properties in good condition and keeping accurate records, investing in properties that offer tax benefits, investing in properties that offer cash flow, staying informed about the local market conditions, building a strong team of professionals, having a long-term vision and a plan in place, having a good understanding of the financing options, investing in properties that offer appreciation potential, being aware of the local rental market conditions, and having a good understanding of the tax implications of owning rental properties, diversifying your portfolio, investing in properties that offer cash flow positive, investing in properties that have the potential for value-add, investing in properties that offer a steady stream of income, and having a friendly attitude and communicating effectively with tenants and other stakeholders, you can reduce risk and increase your income and achieve financial freedom.

It's also important to remember that owning rental properties is a business, and like any business, it takes time, effort and patience to succeed. It's important to keep learning, keep growing and keep diversifying your portfolio. With the right mindset, strategies and a long-term vision you can achieve financial freedom and live the life you've always dreamed of.

Another important aspect to consider when building a rental portfolio is to invest in properties that offer cash flow positive. This means that the rental income generated from the properties is greater than the expenses incurred in maintaining and managing them. This can be achieved by investing in properties that are priced right, located in areas with high demand for rental and by managing them efficiently.

Another important strategy for building a rental portfolio is to invest in properties that have the potential for value-add. This can include properties that need some renovation or improvements to make them more attractive to tenants. By investing in properties that have the potential for value-add, you can increase the rental income and the overall value of the properties in the long run.

When building a rental portfolio, it's also important to have a good understanding of the financing options available to you. This includes understanding the different types of loans, such as conventional loans, FHA loans, VA loans, and others, as well as understanding the terms, interest rates, and down payment requirements. By understanding the financing options, you can make informed decisions about how to acquire and finance properties.

It's also important to keep in mind that owning rental properties is a long-term commitment and that you need to be prepared to handle unexpected expenses and repairs. To mitigate this risk, it's important to budget for contingencies and to have a reserve fund set aside for unexpected expenses.

In summary, building a rental portfolio is a process that requires patience, skill, and the right strategy. By investing in different types of properties, investing in properties in different locations, investing in properties that offer long-term potential, investing in properties that offer additional income potential, investing in properties that have a high demand for rental, investing in properties that offer cash flow positive, investing in properties that have the potential for value-add, investing in properties that offer a steady stream of income, and having a good understanding of the financing options, you can reduce risk and increase your income and achieve financial freedom.

Another strategy for building a rental portfolio is to invest in properties through real estate funds or REITs. This allows you to invest in a diversified portfolio of properties without the need to purchase, manage, or finance them individually. Real estate funds or REITs are professionally managed and provide investors with an opportunity to earn income from rental properties without the hassle of being a landlord.

It's also important to build a strong relationship with your tenants. By communicating effectively and providing good customer service, you can reduce the risk of vacancies and increase the likelihood of tenants renewing their leases. Building a good reputation as a landlord can also help you attract new tenants and increase the value of your properties.

Another important aspect of building a rental portfolio is to stay informed about the local market conditions. This includes understanding the local economy, employment trends, population growth, and demographic changes. This can help you identify areas with strong rental demand and help you make informed decisions about when to buy and sell properties.

Finally, it's important to have a good understanding of the tax implications of owning rental properties, and to work with a qualified tax professional to minimize your tax liability. This includes understanding the tax deductions and credits available to landlords, and taking advantage of them to reduce your tax liability.

In conclusion, building a rental portfolio is a process that requires patience, skill, and the right strategy. By investing in different types of properties, investing in properties in different locations, investing in properties that offer long-term potential, investing in properties that offer additional income potential, investing in properties that are in need of repair or renovation, investing in properties that have a high demand for rental, partnering and joint ventures, investing in real estate funds or REITs, keeping your properties in good condition and keeping accurate records, investing in properties that offer tax benefits, investing in properties that offer cash flow, staying informed about the local market conditions, building a strong team of professionals, having a long-term vision and a plan in place, having a good understanding of the financing options, investing in properties that offer appreciation potential, being aware of the local rental market conditions, having a good understanding of the tax implications of owning rental properties, diversifying your portfolio, investing in properties that offer cash flow positive, investing in properties that have the potential for value-add, investing in properties that offer a steady stream of income, building a strong relationship with your tenants and working with a qualified tax professional, you can reduce risk and increase your income and achieve financial freedom.

Another important aspect of building a rental portfolio is to have a good understanding of the local rental market conditions. This includes understanding the average rental rates, occupancy rates, and the types of properties in demand. By staying informed about the local rental market, you can make informed decisions about when to buy and sell properties, and how to price your rentals.

Additionally, it's important to have a good understanding of the legal aspects of owning rental properties. This includes understanding the laws and regulations governing rental properties in your area, as well as your rights and responsibilities as a landlord. By understanding the legal aspects of owning rental properties, you can minimize your risk of legal disputes and ensure that your properties are operated in compliance with the law.

Another important aspect of building a rental portfolio is to have a good understanding of the insurance options available to landlords. This includes understanding the types of insurance coverage you need to protect your properties, such as property insurance, liability insurance, and rental income insurance. By understanding the insurance options available to landlords, you can minimize your risk of financial loss and protect your assets.

Finally, it's important to have a good understanding of the exit strategy when building a rental portfolio. This includes understanding when to buy and sell properties, how to price your properties and how to optimize your returns. By having a good understanding of the exit strategy, you can maximize your returns on your investments and achieve financial freedom.

In conclusion, building a rental portfolio is a process that requires patience, skill, and the right strategy. By understanding the local rental market conditions, legal aspects, insurance options and exit strategy in addition to the points previously mentioned, you can reduce risk and increase your income and achieve financial freedom. It's important to continuously educate yourself and stay informed about the market conditions and trends to be able to make the best decisions to achieve your goals.

Another important aspect of building a rental portfolio is to develop a system for screening tenants. This includes running background checks, credit checks, and checking rental history to ensure that you are renting to responsible and reliable tenants. By having a good screening process in place, you can minimize the risk of vacancies, late rent payments and evictions.

It's also important to have a well-drafted lease agreement in place when renting out properties. This includes outlining the terms of the lease, the rights and responsibilities of the landlord and tenant, and the procedures for handling disputes. Having a well-drafted lease agreement can help protect your rights as a landlord and minimize the risk of legal disputes.

Another key aspect of building a rental portfolio is to have a system in place for property management and maintenance. This includes regularly inspecting the properties, ensuring that repairs and maintenance are done in a timely manner, and keeping accurate records of all transactions. By having a good property management and maintenance system in place, you can ensure that your properties are in good condition, attract and retain good tenants, and increase the value of your properties over time.

In addition, it's also important to have a strategy in place for managing your finances when building a rental portfolio.

This includes creating a budget, keeping accurate records of your income and expenses, and having a plan in place for managing cash flow. By having a good financial management strategy in place, you can ensure that your properties are generating positive cash flow and that you are able to meet your financial goals.

In conclusion, building a rental portfolio is a process that requires patience, skill, and the right strategy. By having a well-rounded approach, including understanding the local rental market conditions, legal aspects, insurance options, exit strategy, tenant screening, lease agreements, property management, maintenance, and financial management, you can reduce risk and increase your income and achieve financial freedom.

Another important aspect of building a rental portfolio is to have a solid understanding of the local zoning laws and regulations. This includes understanding the different types of zoning, such as residential, commercial, and industrial, as well as understanding the restrictions on the number of units, the type of use, and building codes. By understanding the local zoning laws and regulations, you can ensure that the properties you invest in are in compliance with the law, and that you are able to rent them out legally.

It's also important to have a good understanding of the local real estate market trends, including the current supply and demand for rental properties, the average rental rates, and the types of properties in demand. By staying informed about the local real estate market trends, you can make informed decisions about when to buy and sell properties, and how to price your rentals.

Another key aspect of building a rental portfolio is to have a system in place for handling tenant complaints and disputes. This includes having a clear communication policy, a process for handling complaints and disputes, and having a good understanding of the local landlord-tenant laws. By having a good system in place for handling tenant complaints and disputes, you can minimize the risk of legal disputes and ensure that your tenants are satisfied with the service you provide.

It's also important to have a long-term strategy when building a rental portfolio. This includes setting clear goals, having a plan in place for achieving those goals, and regularly reviewing and adjusting your strategy as needed. By having a long-term strategy, you can ensure that your rental portfolio is aligned with your overall financial goals and that you are on track to achieve financial freedom.

In conclusion, building a rental portfolio is a complex process that requires patience, skill, and the right strategy. By understanding the local zoning laws and regulations, staying informed about the local real estate market trends, having a system in place for handling tenant complaints and disputes, having a long-term strategy, and following all the points previously mentioned, you can reduce risk and increase your income and achieve financial freedom. It's important to stay informed, adapt to the changes in the market and have a clear plan in place to achieve your goals.

*"A wise investor knows the market, understands the laws, and has a plan for success - build your rental portfolio with this approach and financial freedom will be within reach."*

## Notes

........................................................................................................

........................................................................................................

........................................................................................................

# Chapter 6: Tax Advantages and Legal Considerations: Understanding the Tax and Legal Implications of Owning Rental Properties

Owning rental properties can be a great way to generate passive income and build long-term wealth. However, it's important to understand the tax and legal implications of owning rental properties in order to minimize your liability and maximize your profits. In this chapter, we will explore some of the most important tax advantages and legal considerations that landlords and property managers should be aware of.

**Tax Advantages**

There are a number of tax advantages that come with owning rental properties. One of the most significant is the ability to deduct expenses related to the property, such as mortgage interest, property taxes, and repairs. Additionally, landlords can also depreciate their properties over time, which can provide significant tax savings.

Another important tax advantage is the ability to deduct losses from rental properties. If rental income is less than the expenses associated with the property, landlords can deduct the difference as a loss on their taxes. However, it's important to be aware of the passive loss rules and the at-risk rules, which limit the amount of losses that can be deducted in certain situations.

## Legal Considerations

In addition to tax considerations, landlords and property managers must also be aware of the legal implications of owning rental properties. This includes understanding the rights and responsibilities of landlords and tenants under state and federal law, as well as the legal requirements for eviction and security deposit management.

Landlords are also responsible for ensuring that their properties are safe and habitable. This includes complying with local building codes and health and safety regulations, as well as maintaining the property in good condition.

Another important legal consideration is fair housing laws. Landlords cannot discriminate against tenants based on factors such as race, religion, gender, or disability. Additionally, landlords must comply with local and state laws regarding rent control and eviction procedures.

Owning rental properties can be a great way to generate passive income and build long-term wealth. However, it's important to understand the tax and legal implications of owning rental properties in order to minimize liability and maximize profits. By being aware of tax advantages such as deductions and depreciation, and legal considerations such as fair housing laws and eviction procedures, landlords and property managers can make informed decisions and protect themselves from potential legal and financial issues.

It's always recommended to consult with a tax professional or a lawyer to ensure compliance with the applicable laws and regulations. They can help you to navigate the complex tax and legal landscape and ensure that you are taking advantage of all the tax benefits and regulations related to rental properties ownership.

Sure, here are additional paragraphs on tax advantages and legal considerations when owning rental properties:

Another important tax advantage to consider is the 1031 exchange. This allows landlords to defer paying taxes on the sale of a rental property by using the proceeds to purchase a similar property. This can be a powerful tool for landlords looking to upgrade their properties or acquire more rental units without paying a significant tax bill.

It is important to note that as a landlord, you are responsible for withholding and paying taxes on rental income. You must report rental income on your tax return and pay any taxes owed. Not reporting rental income or failing to pay taxes on it can result in significant penalties and interest.

Another legal consideration that landlords should be aware of is the requirement to disclose any known defects or hazards in the rental property. This is known as a "disclosure obligation" and failure to disclose can result in legal liability. This also includes any information about lead-based paint, if the property was built before 1978.

In addition to state and federal laws, landlords should also be familiar with local laws and regulations that may affect their rental properties. This can include zoning laws, business license requirements, and housing codes.

Finally, landlords should also be aware of insurance requirements when owning rental properties. This includes liability insurance, which can protect landlords against any legal claims or damages resulting from injuries on the property. Landlords should also consider purchasing insurance to cover damage to the property caused by natural disasters or other events.

In conclusion, owning rental properties can be a great way to generate passive income and build long-term wealth, but it's important to understand the tax and legal implications of owning rental properties in order to minimize liability and maximize profits. By being aware of tax advantages such as deductions and depreciation, legal considerations such as fair housing laws and eviction procedures, and other important considerations such as disclosing known defects and obtaining insurance, landlords and property managers can make informed decisions and protect themselves from potential legal and financial issues.

Sure, here are some additional paragraphs on tax advantages and legal considerations when owning rental properties:

Another important tax advantage for landlords to consider is the opportunity to deduct a portion of the cost of purchasing, improving, or maintaining a rental property. This is known as the capital cost allowance (CCA) and it allows landlords to deduct a portion of the cost of the property over a period of time, depending on the class of the property. This includes things like the cost of new appliances, new roof, flooring and other repairs and improvements.

It is also important for landlords to be aware of the rules surrounding short-term rentals, also known as vacation rentals. Many localities have specific regulations for short-term rentals and landlords may be required to obtain a permit or register the property with the city. In addition, landlords may be required to collect and remit hotel taxes and/or tourist taxes on behalf of their guests.

In addition, landlords should also be aware of the laws surrounding security deposits. Each state has its own laws surrounding how security deposits are handled, how much can be charged, and how they must be returned to the tenant. This includes rules surrounding the timing of the deposit, interest that may be earned, and how disputes over the deposit are handled.

Another legal consideration landlords should be aware of is the requirement to abide by the terms of any mortgage or loan on the property. This includes making payments on time and maintaining the property in accordance with any terms specified in the loan agreement. Failure to do so can result in foreclosure or other legal action by the lender.

In conclusion, owning rental properties can be a great way to generate passive income and build long-term wealth, but it's important to understand the tax and legal implications of owning rental properties in order to minimize liability and maximize profits. By being aware of tax advantages such as deductions and depreciation, legal considerations such as fair housing laws, security deposit laws and eviction procedures, and other important considerations such as disclosing known defects, obtaining insurance, and complying with local laws, landlords and property managers can make informed decisions and protect themselves from potential legal and financial issues. It's always recommended to consult with a tax professional or a lawyer to ensure compliance with the applicable laws and regulations.

Sure, here are some additional paragraphs on tax advantages and legal considerations when owning rental properties:

Another important legal consideration landlords should be aware of is the requirement to comply with state and federal laws regarding habitability. This includes ensuring that the rental property is free from mold, pests, and other health hazards, and providing proper sanitation and heating facilities. Landlords are also required to provide working smoke detectors and carbon monoxide alarms in the rental units, and must also comply with any additional regulations from the local fire department.

Another important legal consideration for landlords is the requirement to provide proper notice for entry and termination of the tenancy. Landlords must provide proper notice to enter the rental unit, and can only do so for specific reasons such as maintenance or inspection. Landlords must also provide proper notice for termination of the tenancy, and must follow the rules and procedures outlined in the state and local laws.

Lastly, landlords should also be aware of their responsibilities regarding renters insurance. While it is not a legal requirement, many landlords require their tenants to have renters insurance as a condition of the lease. This can protect the landlord from potential liability in the event of a loss or damage to the tenant's personal property. Landlords should also consider purchasing insurance to cover any potential losses that may occur during the tenancy.

In conclusion, owning rental properties can be a great way to generate passive income and build long-term wealth, but it's important to understand the tax and legal implications of owning rental properties in order to minimize liability and maximize profits. By being aware of tax advantages such as deductions and depreciation, legal considerations such as fair housing laws, security deposit laws and eviction procedures, and other important considerations such as disclosing known defects, obtaining insurance, complying with local laws, and compliance with state and federal.

*"Maximizing rental income requires understanding the market, setting the right rent prices, increasing occupancy, and improving the overall appeal of properties."*

## Notes

..............................................................................................................

..............................................................................................................

..............................................................................................................

# Chapter 7: Financing Your Rental Business: Options for Funding Your Rental Business and Managing Cash Flow

Starting and growing a rental business can be expensive. You will need money to buy or fix up properties, pay for expenses, and have a cushion for unexpected events. There are different ways to get the money you need, which are called financing options. In this chapter, we will go over different ways to finance your rental business and manage your money.

**Traditional Mortgages**

One common way to finance a rental business is by getting a traditional mortgage. A traditional mortgage is a loan you get from a bank or other financial institution to buy a property. The property is used as collateral, which means the bank can take it if you don't make your payments. Mortgages usually have a low interest rate and can be paid back over a long period of time.

**Private Loans**

Another financing option is getting a private loan. A private loan is a loan from an individual or a private company, instead of a bank. These loans can be easier to get, but the interest rate is usually higher. Also, private loans are usually short-term loans, which means you have to pay them back faster.

## Alternative Financing Options

There are also alternative financing options, such as crowdfunding or joint ventures. Crowdfunding is when you get money from a lot of people, usually through the internet. Joint ventures are when you team up with another person or company to buy or finance a property. These options can be harder to get, but they can also be more flexible and have less strict requirements.

## Managing Cash Flow

Managing cash flow means making sure you have enough money coming in to pay your bills and have some extra for unexpected events. One way to manage cash flow is to have a budget. A budget is a plan that shows how much money you will earn and how much you will spend. Having a budget can help you make sure you have enough money coming in to pay your bills and have some extra for unexpected events.

Another way to manage cash flow is to have a reserve fund. A reserve fund is a separate account where you put money aside for unexpected events such as repairs or vacancies. Having a reserve fund can help you weather unexpected events without having to borrow money or dip into your profits.

You should also consider setting up a system for tracking your income and expenses. This can be done through the use of software or a spreadsheet, and will help you to stay on top of your cash flow and expenses.

Finally, it's important to always be on the lookout for ways to increase your rental income and decrease your expenses. This can include increasing rent prices, finding ways to save on utilities, and being vigilant about keeping your properties in good condition. By managing your cash flow effectively, you can ensure that your rental business is financially stable and can continue to grow.

In conclusion, financing your rental business is an essential step to growing and expanding your business. By exploring options such as traditional mortgages, private loans, and alternative financing options, landlords and property managers can secure the funding they need to acquire and improve properties. Additionally, by implementing effective cash flow management techniques, such as budgeting and setting up a reserve fund, landlords and property managers can ensure that their rental business is financially stable and can continue to grow.

Another important aspect of financing your rental business is understanding the potential risks and rewards associated with different financing options. For example, traditional mortgages offer lower interest rates and longer repayment terms, but they also require a larger down payment and may come with stricter credit requirements. On the other hand, alternative financing options such as private loans or crowdfunding may have higher interest rates and shorter repayment terms, but they may be more flexible and easier to qualify for.

It is also important to be aware of the tax implications of financing your rental business. For example, mortgage interest is tax-deductible, which can help to reduce your overall tax liability. However, it's important to consult with a tax professional to understand the specific tax implications of each financing option and to ensure compliance with all applicable tax laws.

Another way to finance a rental business is using your own savings or using the equity of your primary residence. This can be a good option for landlords who are just starting out or have limited access to traditional financing options. However, this can also be risky, as it ties up personal savings or the equity of your primary residence. Additionally, it is important to consider the potential risks and rewards of this option, and to consult with a financial advisor if you are considering this option.

In addition, it is also important to consider the impact of inflation on your rental business. Inflation can increase the cost of goods and services, which can eat into your profits.

In order to mitigate the impact of inflation, landlords and property managers should consider increasing rent prices and looking for ways to save on expenses.

In conclusion, financing your rental business is a complex process that requires landlords and property managers to weigh the potential risks and rewards associated with different financing options. By understanding the tax implications, potential risks and rewards, and the impact of inflation, landlords and property managers can make informed decisions and secure the funding they need to acquire and improve properties while ensuring the financial stability of their rental business. Consultation with a financial advisor or a tax professional is always recommended to ensure that you are making the best financial decisions for your business.

Another important aspect of financing your rental business is understanding the different types of loans that are available. For example, conventional loans are the most common type of loan used by landlords and property managers. They are usually provided by banks and other financial institutions and are based on the borrower's creditworthiness and the value of the property. However, there are also other types of loans such as FHA loans, VA loans, and USDA loans that are backed by the government and have different requirements and benefits.

Another important aspect to consider is the terms of the loan. The terms of the loan include the interest rate, the length of the loan, and the repayment schedule. It's important to compare the terms of different loans and choose the one that best suits your needs. Longer terms may have lower interest rates, but they also mean that you'll be paying more in interest over the life of the loan.

It is also important to consider the potential for appreciation or depreciation of the property. Appreciation is when the value of the property increases over time and depreciation is when the value of the property decreases over time. It is important to consider the potential for appreciation or depreciation when choosing a property to purchase and when deciding on the terms of the loan.

Finally, it is important to consider the potential for refinancing the loan. Refinancing means paying off the current loan and getting a new one with different terms. This can be a good option if the interest rates have dropped or if your financial situation has improved. However, it can also be a costly option as there are fees associated with refinancing a loan.

In conclusion, financing your rental business is a complex process that requires landlords and property managers to consider various factors such as the different types of loans available, the terms of the loan, the potential for appreciation or depreciation of the property, and the potential for refinancing. It's important to compare the terms of different loans and choose the one that best suits your needs and consult with a financial advisor or a mortgage broker to ensure that you are making the best financial decisions for your business.

Another important aspect of financing your rental business is understanding the different types of lenders that are available. For example, traditional banks and credit unions are the most common type of lender used by landlords and property managers. They offer loans that are backed by the FDIC or the NCUA and are subject to regulations that protect consumers. However, there are also non-traditional lenders such as hard money lenders, private money lenders and online lenders that offer loans with different terms and requirements.

Another important aspect to consider is the credit requirements of the lender. Traditional banks and credit unions usually have strict credit requirements, which may make it harder for landlords and property managers with less than perfect credit to qualify for a loan. On the other hand, non-traditional lenders such as hard money lenders and private money lenders may have more relaxed credit requirements but may also charge higher interest rates and fees.

It's also important to consider the pre-payment penalties of the loan. Pre-payment penalties are fees that some lenders charge if you pay off the loan early. This can be a costly option and should be considered when choosing a lender and loan terms.

Another important aspect to consider is the type of property you're financing. Different types of properties may have different financing options available. For example, single-family homes, multi-unit properties, and commercial properties all have different financing options available. It is important to research the different options available for the type of property you are looking to finance.

In conclusion, financing your rental business is a complex process that requires landlords and property managers to consider various factors such as the different types of lenders available, the credit requirements of the lender, the pre-payment penalties, and the type of property you're financing. It's important to research the different options available for the type of property you are looking to finance and consult with a financial advisor or a mortgage broker to ensure that you are making the best financial decisions for your business. It's also important to compare the terms of different loans and choose the one that best suits your needs and goals.

Another important aspect of financing your rental business is understanding the different types of rental property financing. For example, traditional rental property financing is typically done through a conventional mortgage loan, which is a loan that is secured by the property and is based on the borrower's creditworthiness and the value of the property. However, there are also other types of rental property financing such as portfolio loans, bridge loans, and hard money loans.

Portfolio loans are loans that are held by the lender rather than being sold on the secondary market. These loans typically have more flexible terms and can be tailored to the specific needs of the borrower. Bridge loans, on the other hand, are short-term loans that are designed to bridge the gap between the purchase of a property and the permanent financing.

Hard money loans are another type of rental property financing that is typically used for fix and flip or short-term rental properties. These loans are based on the value of the property rather than the creditworthiness of the borrower and are typically used for properties that are in need of repairs or renovations.

Another important aspect to consider is the interest rate of the loan. Interest rates can vary depending on the lender, the loan type, and the creditworthiness of the borrower. It's important to compare the interest rates of different loans and choose the one that best suits your needs.

It is also important to consider the fees associated with the loan. Different lenders may charge different fees such as origination fees, application fees, and closing costs. It's important to compare the fees of different loans and choose the one that best suits your needs.

In conclusion, financing your rental business is a complex process that requires landlords and property managers to consider various factors such as the different types of rental property financing, the interest rate of the loan, and the fees associated with the loan. It's important to research the different options available for the type of property you are looking to finance and consult with a financial advisor or a mortgage broker to ensure that you are making the best financial decisions for your business. It's also important to compare the terms of different loans and choose the one that best suits your needs and goals. It's also recommended to have a good understanding of the local real estate market and to have a clear business plan in place.

Another important aspect of financing your rental business is understanding the different types of rental property investments. For example, a rental property can be a long-term rental property, where the tenant rents the property for a long period of time, or it can be a short-term rental property, such as a vacation rental or a short-term corporate rental. The type of rental property investment will have an impact on the financing options available and the cash flow of the property.

Long-term rental properties tend to have more stable cash flow, as the tenants are committed to a long-term lease. This type of rental property investment is typically financed with a traditional mortgage loan. On the other hand, short-term rental properties, such as vacation rentals or corporate rentals, tend to have more fluctuating cash flow as the occupancy rates can vary. Financing options for these types of properties can include traditional mortgages, short-term loans, or lines of credit.

Another important aspect to consider is the location of the rental property. The location of the rental property can have a significant impact on the rental income and the financing options available. Properties located in high-demand areas tend to have higher rental income and may qualify for more favorable financing options. Properties located in less desirable areas may have lower rental income and may be harder to finance.

It's also important to consider the condition of the property. Properties that are in good condition and are move-in ready will typically be easier to finance and may have higher rental income. Properties that are in need of repairs or renovations may be harder to finance and may have lower rental income until the repairs or renovations are completed.

In conclusion, financing your rental business is a complex process that requires landlords and property managers to consider various factors such as the different types of rental property investments, the location of the rental property, and the condition of the property. It's important to research the different options available for the type of property you are looking to finance and consult with a financial advisor or a mortgage broker to ensure that you are making the best financial decisions for your business. It's also important to have a clear understanding of the local real estate market and to have a well-thought-out business plan in place. Additionally, it's important to consider how the type of rental property investment and location can impact the rental income and the financing options available.

*"Financing your rental business requires careful consideration of different options and potential risks and rewards"*

## Notes

..................................................................................................

..................................................................................................

..................................................................................................

# Chapter 8: Conclusion: Achieving Financial Freedom through Real Estate Rentals - Tips, Trick and Best practices

Real estate rentals can be a powerful tool for achieving financial freedom. By carefully managing your properties and tenants, you can create a steady stream of passive income that can help you achieve your financial goals. In this chapter, we will summarize some of the key takeaways from the previous chapters and provide some tips, tricks, and best practices for achieving financial freedom through real estate rentals.

**Tips for Maximizing Rental Income**

Understand the market: The key to maximizing rental income is understanding the local real estate market. By staying informed about local rental rates, you can ensure that you are charging the right price for your properties.

Set the right rent prices: Setting the right rent prices is crucial for maximizing rental income. You want to charge enough to cover your expenses and make a profit, but not so much that your properties are not competitive.

Increase occupancy: The more tenants you have, the more rental income you will generate. By keeping your properties in good condition and marketing them effectively, you can increase occupancy and maximize rental income.

Improve the overall appeal of properties: By making improvements to your properties, such as updating appliances, painting, or adding landscaping, you can increase the overall appeal of your properties and attract higher-paying tenants.

## Tips for Managing Cash Flow

Create a budget: A budget is a plan that shows how much money you will earn and how much you will spend. Having a budget can help you make sure you have enough money coming in to pay your bills and have some extra for unexpected events.

Set up a reserve fund: A reserve fund is a separate account where you put money aside for unexpected events such as repairs or vacancies. Having a reserve fund can help you weather unexpected events without having to borrow money or dip into your profits.

Track income and expenses: Setting up a system for tracking your income and expenses can help you stay on top of your cash flow and expenses. This can be done through the use of software or a spreadsheet.

Look for ways to increase rental income and decrease expenses: Always be on the lookout for ways to increase your rental income and decrease your expenses. This can include increasing rent prices, finding ways to save on utilities, and being vigilant about keeping your properties in good condition.

Tips for Understanding Tax Advantages and Legal Considerations

Consult with a tax professional: It is important to consult with a tax professional to understand the specific tax implications of owning rental properties and to ensure compliance with all applicable tax laws.

Understand depreciation: Depreciation is a tax benefit that allows landlords to deduct a portion of the cost of the property over time. This can help to reduce your overall tax liability.

Keep good records: Keeping accurate and detailed records of your rental income and expenses is essential for tax purposes. This will help you to claim deductions and credits that you are entitled to.

Understand local laws and regulations: Every state and municipality has its own laws and regulations regarding rental properties. It is important to understand these laws and regulations to ensure that you are operating within the legal boundaries.

## Tips for Financing Your Rental Business

Explore all options: There are many different financing options available for rental properties, including traditional mortgages, private loans, and alternative financing options. It is important to explore all options and choose the one that best suits your needs.

Understand the potential risks and rewards: Each financing option has its own potential risks and rewards. It is important to understand these potential risks and rewards before making a decision.

Have a well-thought-out business plan: Having a well-thought-out business plan is essential for securing financing for your rental business. Lenders will want to see that you have a clear plan for how you will generate income and manage expenses.

In conclusion, achieving financial freedom through real estate rentals is a process that requires a combination of careful planning, effective management, and a sound understanding of the local real estate market. By following the tips, tricks, and best practices outlined in this chapter, landlords and property managers can create a steady stream of passive
income that can help them achieve their financial goals. It is important to always be aware of the market trends, understand the local laws and regulations, and have a clear

business plan in place. Additionally, it's important to always be looking for ways to maximize rental income, improve cash flow, and take advantage of tax benefits.

One of the key takeaways from this chapter is that real estate rentals can be a powerful tool for achieving financial freedom, but it requires a lot of effort and dedication. It is important to be patient, persistent and disciplined in your approach. You should always be looking for ways to improve your properties and increase your rental income.

Another key takeaway is the importance of having a strong financial foundation. This includes having a budget, a reserve fund and tracking your income and expenses. This will help you to be prepared for unexpected events and to make informed decisions about your rental business.

Finally, it's important to always be learning and keeping up to date with the latest trends and best practices in the real estate rental market. This can be achieved through attending seminars and workshops, reading books and industry publications, and networking with other landlords and property managers.

In conclusion, achieving financial freedom through real estate rentals is a challenging but rewarding journey that requires a combination of hard work, patience, and dedication. By following the tips, tricks, and best practices outlined in this chapter, landlords and property managers can create a steady stream of passive income that can help them achieve their financial goals. And the key is to always be aware of the market trends, understand the local laws and regulations, have a clear business plan in place and have a strong financial foundation.

Another important aspect to consider when achieving financial freedom through real estate rentals is the importance of property management. Properly managing your properties can mean the difference between a profitable and unprofitable rental business. This includes tasks such as:

Marketing your properties: Properly marketing your properties will ensure that they are seen by a large audience of potential tenants. This can include listing your properties on various rental websites, advertising in local newspapers and magazines, and holding open houses.

Screening tenants: Properly screening tenants can help to reduce the risk of dealing with problem tenants. This includes checking their credit history, employment history, and references.

Handling maintenance and repairs: Keeping your properties in good condition is essential for maintaining high occupancy rates and attracting high-paying tenants. This includes handling routine maintenance and repairs, as well as dealing with any emergency repairs that may arise.

Collecting rent: Collecting rent on time is essential for maintaining positive cash flow. This includes setting up a system for collecting rent, such as online payments or automatic bank drafts, and enforcing late fees for tenants who pay rent late.

Communication with tenants: Regular communication with tenants is essential for maintaining good relationships and addressing any issues that may arise. This includes sending out regular newsletters, holding tenant meetings, and responding to tenant complaints in a timely manner.

By properly managing your properties, landlords and property managers can ensure that their rental business is profitable and sustainable. This includes maintaining the property, attracting and retaining tenants, and ensuring that the rental business is running smoothly.

In conclusion, achieving financial freedom through real estate rentals is a complex process that requires landlords and property managers to consider various factors such as maximizing rental income, managing cash flow, understanding tax advantages and legal considerations, and financing the rental business.

Additionally, it's important to understand the importance of property management and the role it plays in ensuring the profitability and sustainability of the rental business. By following the tips, tricks, and best practices outlined in this chapter, landlords and property managers can create a steady stream of passive income that can help them achieve their financial goals. However, it's important to always be aware that it's a continuous effort to stay up to date with the market trends, laws and regulations, and to be proactive in managing the properties, attracting and retaining tenants, and ensuring that the rental business is running smoothly.

Another important aspect to consider is the long-term strategy for the rental business. This includes setting long-term goals such as increasing the number of properties in the portfolio, diversifying the types of properties, and considering options such as renting out commercial properties. Having a long-term strategy in place can help landlords and property managers to make informed decisions and ensure that the rental business is aligned with their overall financial goals.

It's also important to have a good understanding of the real estate market and to have a well-thought-out investment strategy. This includes researching different markets, understanding property values, and identifying the best areas to invest in. It's also essential to have a good understanding of the real estate market trends, including the current state of the economy and any potential changes that may affect the rental market.

In conclusion, achieving financial freedom through real estate rentals is a continuous effort that requires landlords and property managers to consider various factors such as maximizing rental income, managing cash flow, understanding tax advantages and legal considerations, financing the rental business, property management and having a long-term strategy in place. It's important to always be aware of the market trends, laws and regulations, and to be proactive in managing the properties, attracting and retaining tenants, and ensuring that the rental business is running smoothly, and to have a good understanding of the real estate market and to have a well-thought-out investment strategy.

Another important aspect of achieving financial freedom through real estate rentals is building a team of professionals to help you manage your business. This includes hiring a property management company, an accountant, and a real estate attorney. A property management company can help with tasks such as marketing, screening tenants, collecting rent, and handling maintenance and repairs. An accountant can help with tax planning and compliance, and a real estate attorney can advise on legal matters and help to protect your interests.

Additionally, it's also important to have a good insurance coverage for your rental properties. This includes liability insurance, which protects you from claims made by tenants or visitors, and property insurance, which covers damage to the property from natural disasters or other unexpected events. It's also recommended to have insurance for loss of income, which covers the income loss if the property is uninhabitable due to damages.

Another important aspect to consider is building a strong online presence for your rental business. This includes having a website, social media accounts, and online listings for your properties. This can help to increase the visibility of your properties and attract potential tenants.

Lastly, it's important to continuously educate yourself and stay up to date with the latest trends and best practices in the real estate rental market. This can include attending seminars and workshops, reading books and industry publications, and networking with other landlords and property managers.

In conclusion, achieving financial freedom through real estate rentals is a continuous effort that requires landlords and property managers to consider various factors such as maximizing rental income, managing cash flow, understanding tax advantages and legal considerations, financing the rental business, property management, having a long-term strategy in place, building a team of professionals, having a good insurance coverage, building a strong online presence, and continuously educating yourself and staying up to date with the latest trends and best practices in the real estate rental market.

Another important aspect of achieving financial freedom through real estate rentals is the ability to scale your rental business. This includes strategies such as acquiring more properties, diversifying your portfolio by investing in different types of properties and markets, and increasing the number of units in a multi-unit building. By scaling your rental business, you can increase your rental income and achieve greater financial freedom.

Another strategy to consider is the use of leverage, which allows you to acquire properties without using all of your own money. This can include using a mortgage, a home equity loan, or a line of credit to purchase properties. However, it's important to be aware that leverage can also increase your risk, so it's important to have a good understanding of the market conditions and your ability to manage the risk before using leverage.

Another effective strategy for achieving financial freedom through real estate rentals is creating passive income streams. This can include renting out storage units, parking spaces, and other non-residential properties. Additionally, creating passive income streams can also include developing ancillary businesses that are related to your rental properties, such as starting a property management company, a cleaning service, or a handyman service.

In conclusion, achieving financial freedom through real estate rentals is a continuous effort that requires landlords and property managers to consider various factors such as maximizing rental income, managing cash flow, understanding tax advantages and legal considerations, financing the rental business, property management, having a long-term strategy in place, building a team of professionals, having a good insurance coverage, building a strong online presence, continuously educating yourself and staying up to date with the latest trends and best practices in the real estate rental market, scaling your rental business, using leverage and creating passive income streams. It's important to be aware of the market conditions and to have a well thought out strategy to increase the rental income and achieve greater financial freedom.

Another important aspect of achieving financial freedom through real estate rentals is the ability to manage and minimize risks. This includes strategies such as diversifying your portfolio by investing in different types of properties and markets, spreading out your investments across different geographical regions, and having a good understanding of the local market conditions. Additionally, it's important to have a good understanding of the potential risks associated with owning rental properties and to have a plan in place to manage these risks.

Another strategy to minimize risk is to have a good understanding of the tenant profile, such as their creditworthiness, employment history, and references. This can help to reduce the risk of dealing with problem tenants and increase the likelihood of having stable and long-term tenants.

Another important aspect of risk management is to have a good understanding of the local laws and regulations related to rental properties and to ensure that you are in compliance with all the regulations. This includes understanding the eviction laws and procedures, and having a good understanding of the Fair Housing Act and other laws that protect tenants' rights.

It's also important to have a good understanding of the insurance options available for rental properties and to ensure that you have the right coverage in place. This includes liability insurance, which protects you from claims made by tenants or visitors, and property insurance, which covers damage to the property from natural disasters or other unexpected events.

In conclusion, achieving financial freedom through real estate rentals is a continuous effort that requires landlords and property managers to consider various factors such as maximizing rental income, managing cash flow, understanding tax advantages and legal considerations, financing the rental business, property management, having a long-term strategy in place, building a team of professionals, having a good insurance coverage, building a strong online presence, continuously educating yourself and staying up to date with the latest trends and best practices in the real estate rental market, scaling your rental business, using leverage, creating passive income streams and managing and minimizing risks by diversifying your portfolio, having a good understanding of the tenant profile, understanding the local laws and regulations, and having the right insurance coverage in place.

Another important aspect of achieving financial freedom through real estate rentals is the ability to manage and minimize costs. This includes strategies such as finding ways to save on utilities, maintenance and repairs, property management fees, and other expenses associated with owning rental properties. Additionally, it's important to have a good understanding of the costs associated with owning rental properties and to have a plan in place to manage these costs.

One way to minimize costs is to have a good understanding of the local real estate market and to negotiate the best deals when buying properties. This includes understanding the property values, the potential for appreciation and the rental income potential. It's also important to negotiate the best terms for mortgages, home equity loans, and other forms of financing.

Another way to minimize costs is to have a good understanding of the local laws and regulations related to rental properties and to ensure that you are in compliance with all the regulations. This includes understanding the eviction laws and procedures, and having a good understanding of the Fair Housing Act and other laws that protect tenants' rights. It's also important to be aware of any tax benefits or deductions available and to take advantage of these to minimize costs.

In conclusion, achieving financial freedom through real estate rentals is a continuous effort that requires landlords and property managers to consider various factors such as maximizing rental income, managing cash flow, understanding tax advantages and legal considerations, financing the rental business, property management, having a long-term strategy in place, building a team of professionals, having a good insurance coverage, building a strong online presence, continuously educating yourself and staying up to date with the latest trends and best practices in the real estate rental market, scaling your rental business, using leverage, creating passive income streams, managing and minimizing risks by diversifying your portfolio, having a good understanding of the tenant profile, understanding the local laws and regulations, and having the right insurance coverage in place and managing and minimizing costs by understanding the local real estate market, negotiating the best deals, understanding the local laws and regulations, taking advantage of any tax benefits or deductions available.

Another important aspect of achieving financial freedom through real estate rentals is the ability to adapt to changes in the market. This includes understanding the economic conditions, demographic changes, and other factors that can impact the rental market. Additionally, it's important to have a good understanding of the potential changes that may affect the rental market and to have a plan in place to adapt to these changes.

One way to adapt to changes in the market is to stay informed about the latest trends and best practices in the real estate rental market. This includes attending seminars and workshops, reading books and industry publications, and networking with other landlords and property managers. By staying informed, landlords and property managers can be better prepared to adapt to changes in the market and take advantage of new opportunities.

Another way to adapt to changes in the market is to diversify your portfolio. This includes investing in different types of properties and markets, and having a mix of long-term and short-term rentals. By diversifying your portfolio, landlords and property managers can be better prepared to adapt to changes in the market and take advantage of new opportunities.

Another way to adapt to changes in the market is to be flexible with your rental prices. This includes being willing to adjust your rental prices based on market conditions, such as supply and demand, and being willing to negotiate with tenants on rent prices and lease terms.

In conclusion, achieving financial freedom through real estate rentals is a continuous effort that requires landlords and property managers to consider various factors such as maximizing rental income, managing cash flow, understanding tax advantages and legal considerations, financing the rental business, property management, having a long-term strategy in place, building a team of professionals, having a good insurance coverage, building a strong online presence, continuously educating yourself and staying up to date with the latest trends and best practices in the real estate rental market, scaling your rental business, using leverage, creating passive income streams, managing and minimizing risks by diversifying your portfolio, having a good understanding of the tenant profile, understanding the local laws and regulations, and having the right insurance coverage in place, managing and minimizing costs, and adapting to changes in the market by staying informed about the latest trends and best practices, diversifying your portfolio, and being flexible with your rental prices.

*"Achieving financial freedom through real estate rentals requires a continuous effort in managing and maximizing income, understanding tax and legal implications, proper financing and property management, while being adaptable to market changes and minimizing risks."*

## Notes

..................................................................................

..................................................................................

..................................................................................

# THE END

Achieving financial freedom through real estate rentals is a process that requires landlords and property managers to consider various factors such as maximizing rental income, managing cash flow, understanding tax advantages and legal considerations, financing the rental business, property management, long-term strategies, real estate market trends, legal and tax implications, insurance, scaling your rental business, creating passive income streams, minimizing risks, costs and adapting to changes in the market. This book has provided a comprehensive overview of the strategies and best practices needed to build a successful rental business. By following the advice and strategies outlined in this book, landlords and property managers can achieve their financial goals and create a steady stream of passive income through real estate rentals. Remember to always consult with professionals, stay informed and adapt to changes in the market. We wish you all the best in your journey towards financial freedom through real estate rentals.

We hope that you enjoyed reading the book, and if you have learned anything from this book, and found it helpful, please review the book on Amazon.

.

Thanks!

**Rent to Wealth: The Proven Path to Financial Freedom through Rental Property**

www.ingramcontent.com/pod-product-compliance
Lightning Source LLC
Chambersburg PA
CBHW020656220526
45464CB00001B/462